Where We Got the Bible

Where We Got the Bible

Our Debt
to the
Catholic Church

Henry G. Graham

Catholic Answers
SAN DIEGO

Nihil Obstat and Imprimatur:

> Rev. John Ritchie
> Vicar General
> Glasgow

The Nihil Obstat and *Imprimatur* are official declarations that a book is considered to be free of doctrinal or moral error. No implication is contained therein that those who have granted the *Nihil Obstat* or the *Imprimatur* agree with the contents, opinions, or statements expressed.

Published by Catholic Answers, Inc.
P.O. Box 17490
San Diego, CA 92177

Cover design by Tammi Shore/Shore Design Associates
Printed in the United States of America
ISBN 1-888992-04-2

Contents

Foreword

HENRY G. GRAHAM was born in 1874, the son of a minister in the Presbyterian Church of Scotland. When he was twenty-nine he was received into the Catholic Church, and in 1906 he was ordained in the Lateran Basilica by Cardinal Respighi. Returning to Scotland the following year, he engaged in parish work in the Motherwell Diocese and in 1917 was consecrated auxiliary bishop of the Archdiocese of St. Andrews and Edinburgh. He held that position until 1930, when, a younger archbishop having been appointed, he moved to Glasgow, spending his retirement years as a parish priest. He died in 1959.

Not long after his ordination Graham presented a series of lectures on the Bible and its origin. These lectures were expanded and appeared in the Catholic press during 1908–1909. They were modified further and issued in 1911 as *Where We Got the Bible*, the publication coinciding with the tercentenary of the Authorized (or King James) Version. Graham explained that, "amid the flood of literature on the subject of the Bible, it seemed but right that some statement, however plain and simple, should be set forth from the Catholic side, with the object of bringing home to the average mind the debt that Britain, in common with the rest of Christendom, owes to the Catholic Church in this connection."

Since its first publication, *Where We Got the Bible* seems never to have gone out of print. This modest work, dedicated to "all lovers of the written Word of God," has been instrumental in confirming

Catholics in their faith and in leading "Bible Christians" to a better understanding of the role played by the Catholic Church in forming, preserving, and disseminating Scripture. No one who reads the book will be able to rest comfortably in the fiction that the Church in any way "opposed" the Bible.

Preceding the appearance of *Where We Got the Bible* by about a year was Graham's conversion story, *From the Kirk to the Catholic Church*. A moving account of his interior struggles as a Calvinist minister attracted to Rome, the essay was reprinted in 1960 by the Catholic Truth Society of Scotland but then seems to have been forgotten. Catholic Answers serendipitously came upon the text, ran it in *This Rock* magazine in 1995, and here joins it to Graham's better-known work.

The result is a two-in-one book that exonerates the Catholic Church from the charge of neglecting the Bible and that shows how the truth of the faith can reach even someone reared in a society burdened with centuries of anti-Catholic prejudice.

Karl Keating
President
Catholic Answers

1

Some Errors Removed

IN ORDER TO UNDERSTAND properly the work of the Catholic
Church in creating and defending and perpetuating the Holy
Scriptures, we must say a few preliminary words as to the human
means used in their production and in the collecting of the books
of the Bible as we have it at present. There are common erroneous
ideas which we would do well to clear away from our minds at the
very outset.

1. To begin with, the Bible did not drop down from heaven
ready made, as some seem to imagine; it did not suddenly appear
upon the earth, carried down from Almighty God by the hand of
angel or seraph; but it was written by men like ourselves, who held
in their hand pen (or reed) and ink and parchment and laboriously
traced every letter in the original languages of the East. They were
divinely inspired certainly, as no others ever have been before or
since; nevertheless they were human beings, men chosen by God
for the work, making use of the human instruments that lay to their
hand at the time.

2. In the second place we shall do well to remember that the
Bible was not written all at once or by one man, like most other
books with which we are acquainted, but that 1,500 years elapsed
between the writing of Genesis (the first book of the Old Testament)
and the Apocalypse or Revelation of John (the last book of the
New). It is made up of a collection of different books by different
authors, forming, in short, a library instead of a single work, and

hence called in Greek "*biblia*" or "the books." If you had lived in the days immediately succeeding the death of Moses, all you would have had given to you to represent the Bible would have been the first five books of the Old Testament, written by that patriarch himself; that was the Bible in embryo, so to speak—the little seed that was to grow subsequently into a great tree, the first stone laid on which was gradually to be erected the beautiful temple of the written Word throughout the centuries that followed.

From this we can see that the preacher extolling the Bible as the only comfort and guide of faithful souls was slightly out of his reckoning when he used these words: "Ah, my brethren! What was it that comforted and strengthened Joseph in his dark prison in Egypt? What was it that formed his daily support and meditation? What but that blessed book, the Bible!" As Joseph existed before a line of the Old Testament was penned, and about 1,800 years before the first of the New Testament books saw the light, the worthy evangelist was guilty of what we call a slight anachronism.

3. Nor will it be out of place to remark here that the Bible was not written originally in English or Gaelic. Some folks speak as if they believed that the sacred books were first composed, and the incomparable psalms of David set forth, in the sweet English tongue, and that they were afterwards rendered into barbarous language such as Latin or Greek or Hebrew for the sake of inquisitive scholars and critics. This is not correct; the original language, broadly speaking, of the Old Testament was Hebrew; that of the New Testament was Greek. Thus our Bibles as we have them today for reading are "translations"—that is, are a rendering or equivalent in English of the original Hebrew and Greek as it came from the pen of prophet and apostle and evangelist. We see this plainly enough in the title-page of the Protestant New Testament, which reads "New Testament of Our Lord and Savior Jesus Christ, translated out of the original Greek."

4. A last point must always be kept clearly in mind, for it concerns one of the greatest delusions entertained by Protestants and makes their fierce attacks on Rome appear so silly and irrational —the point, namely, that the Bible, as we have it now, was not

printed in any language at all till about 1,500 years after the birth of Christ, for the simple reason that there was no such thing as printing known before that date. We have become so accustomed to the use of the printing press that we can scarcely conceive of the ages when the only books known to men were in handwriting; but it is the fact that, had we lived and flourished before Johann Gutenberg discovered the art of printing in the fifteenth century, we should have had to read our Testaments and our Gospels from the manuscript of monk or friar, from the pages of parchment or vellum or paper covered with the handwriting, sometimes very beautiful and ornamental, of the scribe that had undertaken the slow and laborious task of copying the sacred Word.

Protestants in these days send shiploads of printed Bibles abroad, and scatter thousands of Testaments hither and thither in every direction for the purpose of evangelizing the heathen and converting sinners, and declare that the Bible, and the Bible only, can save men's souls. What, then, came of those poor souls who lived before the Bible was printed, before it was even written in its present form? How were nations made familiar with the Christian religion and converted to Christianity before the fifteenth century?

Our divine Lord, I suppose, wished that the unnumbered millions of human creatures born before the year 1500 should believe what he had taught and save their souls and go to heaven, at least as much as those of the sixteenth and twentieth centuries; but how could they do this when they had no Bibles, or were too poor to buy one, or could not read it even though they bought it, or could not understand it even if they could read it?

On the Catholic plan (so to call it) of salvation through the teaching of the Church, souls may be saved and people become saints and believe and do all that Jesus Christ meant them to believe and do—and, as a matter of fact, this has happened—in all countries and in all ages without either the written or the printed Bible, and both before and after its production. The Protestant theory, on the contrary, which stakes a man's salvation on the possession of the Bible, leads to the most flagrant absurdities, imputes to Almighty God a total indifference to the salvation of the countless souls that passed hence to eternity for 1,500 years, and indeed ends logically in the blasphemous conclusion that our Blessed Lord failed to provide an adequate means of conveying to men in every age the knowledge of his truth.

We shall see, as we proceed, the utter impossibility of the survival of Christianity, and of its benefits to humanity, on the principle of "the Bible and the Bible only." Meanwhile we can account for the fact that intelligent non-Catholics have not awakened to its hollowness and absurdity only by supposing that they do not sufficiently realize, "read, mark, learn, and inwardly digest" (as the English Prayer Book says) this single item of history—the Bible was not printed till at least 1,400 years after Christ.

II

The Making of the Old Testament

LOOKING AT THE BIBLE as it stands today, we find it is composed of seventy-three separate books—forty-six in the Old Testament and twenty-seven in the New. How has it come to be composed precisely of these seventy-three and no others, no more and no less? Taking first the Old Testament, we know that it always has been divided into three main portions—the Law, the Prophets, and the Writings. The Law, as I remarked before, was the nucleus, the earliest substantial part, which at one time formed the sole book of Scripture that the Jews possessed. Moses wrote it and placed a copy of it in the Ark; that was about 3,300 years ago. To this were added, long afterwards, the Prophets and the Writings, forming the complete Old Testament. At what date precisely the volume or "canon" of the Old Testament was finally closed and recognized as completed forever is not absolutely certain.

When was the Old Testament compiled? Some would decide for about the year 430 B.C., under Esdras and Nehemiah, resting upon the authority of the famous Jew, Josephus, who lived immediately after our Lord and who declares that since the death of Ataxerxes, 424 B.C., "no one had dared to add anything to the Jewish Scriptures, to take anything from them, or to make any change in them." Other authorities, again, contend that it was not till near 100 B.C. that the Old Testament volume was finally closed by the inclusion of the Writings. But whichever contention is correct, one thing at least is certain, that by this last date—that is, for one hundred years before the birth of our Blessed Lord—the Old Testament existed precisely as we have it now.

Of course, I have been speaking so far of the Old Testament in Hebrew, because it was written by Jewish authority in the Jewish language, namely, Hebrew, for Jews, God's chosen people. But after what is called the "Dispersion" of the Jews, when that people was scattered abroad and settled in many other lands outside Palestine and began to lose their Hebrew tongue and gradually became familiar with Greek, which was then a universal language, it was necessary to furnish them with a copy of their Sacred Scriptures in the Greek language.

Hence arose that translation of the Hebrew Old Testament into Greek known as the Septuagint. This word means in Latin seventy, and is so named because it is supposed to have been the work of seventy translators, who performed their task at Alexandria, where there was a large Greek-speaking colony of Jews. Begun about 280 or 250 years before Christ, we may safely say that it was finished in the next century; it was the acknowledged Bible of all the "Jews of the Dispersion" in Asia, as well as in Egypt, and was the version used by our Lord, his apostles and evangelists, and by Jews and Gentiles and Christians in the early days of Christianity. It is from this version that Jesus Christ and the New Testament writers and speakers quote when referring to the Old Testament.

But what about the Christians in other lands who could not understand Greek? When the gospel had been spread abroad, and many people embraced Christianity through the labors of apostles and missionaries in the first two centuries of our era, naturally they had to be supplied with copies of the Scriptures of the Old Testament (which was the inspired Word of God) in their own tongue; this gave rise to translations of the Bible into Armenian and Syriac and Coptic and Arabic and Ethiopic for the benefit of the Christians in these lands.

For the Christians in Africa, where Latin was best understood, there was a translation of the Bible made into Latin about A.D. 150, and, later, another and better translation for the Christians in Italy; but all these were finally superseded by the grand and most important version made by Jerome in Latin called the "Vulgate"—that is, the common, or current, or accepted version. This was in the fourth century of our era. By the time Jerome was born, there was great need of securing a correct and uniform text in Latin of Holy Scripture, for there was danger, through the variety and corrupt conditions of many translations then existing, lest the pure Scripture should be lost.

So Jerome, who was a monk and perhaps the most learned scholar of his day, at the command of Pope Damasus in 382, made a fresh Latin version of the New Testament (which was by this time practically settled), correcting the existing versions by the earliest Greek manuscripts he could find. Then in his cell at Bethlehem, between (approximately) the years 392–404, he also translated the Old Testament into Latin directly from the Hebrew (not from the Greek Septuagint)—except the Psalter, which he had previously revised from existing Latin versions.

This Bible was the celebrated Vulgate, the official text in the Catholic Church, the value of which all scholars admit to be simply inestimable, and which continued to influence all other versions and to hold the chief place among Christians down to the Reformation. I say the "official" text because the Council of Trent in 1546 issued a decree, stamping it as the only recognized and authoritative version allowed to Catholics. "If anyone does not receive the entire books with all their parts as they are accustomed to be read in the Catholic Church, and in the old Latin Vulgate edition, as sacred and canonical . . . let him be anathema." It was revised under Pope Sixtus V in 1590 and again under Pope Clement VIII in 1593, who is responsible for the present standard text.

It is from the Vulgate that our English Douay Version comes, and it is of this same Vulgate that the commission under Cardinal Gasquet, by command of the Pope, is trying to find or restore the original text as it came from the hands of Jerome, uncorrupted by and stripped of subsequent admixtures with other Latin copies.

III

The Church Precedes the New Testament

S O FAR, WE HAVE BEEN DEALING with rather dry material. We have seen how the Old Testament books came to be collected into one volume; it remains to see how the Catholic Church also composed and selected and formed into another volume the separate books of the New Testament.

1. Now you will remember what I said before, that the New Testament was not, any more than the Old, all written at one time, or all by one man, but that at least forty years passed away between the writing of the first and the writing of the last of its books. It is made up of the four Gospels, fourteen Epistles of Paul, two of Peter, one of James, one of Jude, three of John, together with the Revelation of John and the Acts of the Apostles by Luke, who also wrote the third Gospel; so that we have in this collection works by at least eight different writers, and from the year that the earliest book was composed (probably the Gospel of Matthew) to the year that John composed his Gospel about half a century had elapsed.

While on earth, our Blessed Lord himself never, so far as we know, wrote a line of Scripture—certainly none that has been preserved. He never told his apostles to write anything. He did not command them to commit to writing what he had delivered to them, but he said, "Go ye and teach all nations," "Preach the gospel to every creature," "He that heareth you heareth me."

What he commanded and meant them to do was precisely what he had done himself—deliver the Word of God to the people by

8

the living voice—convince, persuade, instruct, convert them by addressing themselves face to face to living men and women; not entrust their message to a dead book which might perish and be destroyed and be misunderstood and misinterpreted and corrupted, but adopt the more safe and natural way of presenting the truth to them by word of mouth and of training others to do the same after they themselves were gone and so, by a living tradition, preserving and handing down the Word of God, as they had received it, to all generations.

2. This was, as a matter of fact, the method that the apostles adopted. Only five out of the twelve wrote down anything at all that has been preserved to us; and of that, not a line was penned till at least ten years after the death of Christ, for Jesus Christ was crucified in A.D. 33, and the first of the New Testament books was not written till about A.D. 45. You see what follows?

The Church and the faith existed *before* the Bible; that seems an elementary and simple fact which no one can deny or ever has denied. Thousands of people became Christians through the work of the apostles and missionaries of Christ in various lands, and believed the whole truth of God as we believe it now, and became saints, before ever they saw or read, or could possibly see or read, a single sentence of inspired Scripture of the New Testament, for the simple reason that such Scripture did not then exist.

How, then, did they become Christians? In the same way, of course, that pagans become Catholics nowadays, by hearing the truth of God from the lips of Christ's missionaries. When the twelve apostles met together in Jerusalem and portioned out the known world among themselves for purposes of evangelization, allotting one country to one apostle (such as India to Thomas) and another to another, how did they propose to evangelize these people? By presenting each one with a New Testament? Such a thing did not exist and, we may safely say, was not even thought of.

Why did our Lord promise them the gift of the Holy Ghost and command them to be "witnesses" of him, and why, in fact, did the Holy Ghost come down upon the twelve and endow them with the power of speaking in various languages? Why but that they might be able to "preach the gospel to every creature" in the tongue of every creature.

3. I have said that the apostles at first never thought of writing the New Testament. The books of the New Testament were produced and called forth by special circumstances that arose, were written to meet particular demands and emergencies. Nothing was further from the minds of the apostles and evangelists than the idea of composing works which should be collected and formed into one volume and so constitute the Holy Book of the Christians. We can imagine Paul staring in amazement if he had been told that his epistles, and Peter's and John's, and the others would be tied up together and elevated into the position of a complete and exhaustive statement of the doctrines of Christianity, to be placed in each man's hand as an easy and infallible guide in faith and morals, independent of any living and teaching authority to interpret them.

No one would have been more shocked at the idea of his letters usurping the place of the authoritative teacher—the Church—than the great apostle who himself said, "How shall they hear without a preacher? How shall they preach unless they be sent? Faith cometh by hearing, and hearing by the Word of Christ." The fact is that no religion yet known has been effectually propagated among men except by word of mouth, and certainly everything in the natural and spiritual position of the apostles on the one hand, and of the Jews on the other, was utterly unfavorable to the spread of Christianity by means of a written record.

The Jewish people were not used to it, and the Gentiles could not have understood it. Even Protestant authors of the highest standing are compelled to admit that the living teaching of the Church was necessarily the means chosen by Jesus Christ for the spread of his gospel and that the committing of it to writing was a later and secondary development. Dr. Westcott, Bishop of Durham, than whom among Anglicans there is not a higher authority and who is reckoned, indeed, by all as a standard scholar on the canon of Scripture, says (*The Bible in the Church*, pp. 53 and seqq.): "In order to appreciate the apostolic age in its essential character, it is necessary to dismiss not only the ideas which are drawn from a collected New Testament, but those also, in a great measure, which spring from the several groups of writings of which it is composed. The first work of the apostles, and that out of which all their other functions grew, was to deliver in living words a personal testimony to the cardinal facts of the gospel—the ministry, the death, and the Resurrection of our Lord. It was only in the course of time, and under the influence of external circumstances, that they committed their testimony, or any part of it, to writing. Their peculiar duty was to preach. That they did, in fact, perform a mission for all ages in perpetuating the tidings which they delivered was due, not to any conscious design which they formed, nor to any definite command which they received, but to that mysterious power," etc.

"The repeated experience of many ages has even yet hardly sufficed to show that a permanent record of his words and deeds, open to all, must coexist with the living body of the Church, if that is to continue in pure and healthy vigor."

Again: "The apostles, when they speak, claim to speak with divine authority, but they nowhere profess to give in writing a system of Christian doctrine. Gospels and epistles, with the exception perhaps of the writings of John, were called out by special circumstances. There is no trace of any designed connection between the separate books, except in the case of the Gospel of Luke and the Acts (also by Luke), still less of any outward unity or completeness in the entire collection. On the contrary, it is not unlikely that some epistles of Paul have been lost, and though, in point of fact, the books which remain do combine to form a perfect whole, yet the completeness is due not to any conscious cooperation of their authors, but to the will of him by whose power they wrote and wrought."

What a contrast there is, in these words of the great scholar, to the common delusion that seems to have seized some minds—that the Bible, complete and bound, dropped down among the Christians from heaven after the day of Pentecost or, at the least, the twelve apostles sat down together in an upper room, pens in hand, and wrote off at a sitting all the books of the New Testament! Allow me to give one more short quotation to drive home the point

I am laboring at, that the written New Testament could never have been intended as the only means of preaching salvation. "It was some considerable time after our Lord's Ascension" (writes the Protestant author of *Helps to the Study of the Bible*, p. 2), "before any of the books contained in the New Testament were actually written. The first and most important work of the apostles was to deliver a personal testimony to the chief facts of the gospel history. Their teaching was at first *oral*, and it was no part of their intention to create a permanent literature." These, I consider, are valuable admissions.

4. But now, you may say, "What was the use of writing the Gospels and epistles then at all? Did not God inspire men to write them? Are you not belittling and despising God's Word?" No, not at all; we are simply putting it in its proper place, the place that God meant it to have; and I would add, the Catholic Church is the only body in these days which teaches infallibly that the Bible, and the whole of it, *is* the Word of God, and defends its inspiration, and denounces and excommunicates anyone who would dare to impugn its divine origin and authority.

I said before, and I repeat, that the separate books of the New Testament came into being to meet special demands, in response to particular needs, and were not, nor are they now, absolutely necessary either to the preaching or the perpetuating of the gospel of Christ.

It is easy to see how the Gospels arose. So long as the apostles were still living, the necessity for written records of the words and actions of our Lord was not so pressing. But when the time came for their removal from this world, it was highly expedient that some correct, authoritative, reliable account be left of our Lord's life by those who had known him personally or at least were in a position to have firsthand, uncorrupted information concerning it.

This was all the more necessary because there were being spread abroad incorrect, unfaithful, indeed altogether spurious Gospels, which were calculated to injure and ridicule the character and work of our divine Redeemer. Luke distinctly declares that this was what caused him to undertake the writing of his Gospel—"For as much as *many have taken in hand* to set forth in order a narration of the things that have been accomplished among us" (1:1). He goes on to say that he has his information from eyewitnesses, has come to know all particulars from the very beginning, and therefore considers it right to set them down in writing, to secure a correct and trustworthy account of Christ's life.

So Matthew, Mark, Luke, and John penned their Gospels for the use of the Church, the one supplying often what another omits, but yet none pretending to give an exhaustive or perfect account of all that Jesus Christ said and did, for if this had been attempted, John tells us, "the whole world would not have contained the books that would be written" about it. The Gospels, then, are incomplete and fragmentary, giving us certainly the most important things to know about our Savior's earthly life, but still not telling us all we might know or much we do know in fact now and understand better through the teaching of the Catholic Church, which has preserved traditions handed down since the time of the apostles, from one generation to another.

These Gospels were read, as they are now among Catholics, at the gatherings of the Christians in the earliest days on the Sundays —not to set forth a scheme of doctrine that they knew already, but to animate their courage, to excite their love and devotion to Jesus Christ, and impel them to imitate the example of that beloved Master, whose sayings and doings were read aloud in their ears.

Well, now, what I said about the Gospels is equally true of the epistles, which make up practically the whole of the rest of the New Testament. They were called into existence at various times to meet pressing needs and circumstances, were addressed to particular individuals and communities in various places and not to the Catholic Church at large. The thought furthest from the mind of the writers was that they should ever be collected into one volume and made to do duty as a complete and all-sufficient statement of Christian faith and morals. How did they arise? In this natural and simple way. Peter, Paul, and the rest went forth to various lands, preaching the gospel, and made thousands of converts, and in each place founded a church, and left priests in charge, and a bishop sometimes (as, e.g., Timothy in Ephesus). Now these priests and converts had occasion many a time to consult their spiritual father and founder, like Paul, or Peter, or James, on many points of doctrine or discipline or morals, for we must not imagine at that date, when the Church was in its infancy, things were so clearly seen or understood or formulated as they are now.

It was, of course, the same faith then as always, but still there were many points on which the newly made Christians were glad to consult the apostles who had been sent out with the unction of Jesus Christ fresh upon them—points of dogma and ritual and government and conduct which they alone could settle. So we find Paul writing to the Ephesians (his converts at Ephesus), or to the Corinthians (his converts at Corinth), or to the Philippians (his converts at Philippi), and so on to the rest (fourteen epistles in all). For what reason? Either in answer to communications sent to him from them, or because he had heard from other sources that there were some things that required correction in these places.

All manner of topics are dealt with in these letters, sometimes in the most homely style. It might be to advise the converts or to reprove them, to encourage them or instruct them, or to defend himself from false accusations. It might be, like that to Philemon, a letter about a private person as Onesimus, the slave. But whatever the epistles deal with, it is clear as the noonday sun that they were written just at particular times to meet particular cases that occurred naturally in the course of his missionary labors and that neither Paul, nor any of the other apostles, intended by these letters to set forth the whole theology or scheme of Christian salvation any more than Pope Pius X intended to do so in his decree against the Modernists or in his letter on the sanctification of the clergy. The thing seems plain on the face of it.

Leo XIII writes to the Scotch bishops on the Holy Scriptures, for example; or Pius X to the Eucharistic Congress in London on the Blessed Sacrament or publishes a decree on frequent Communion; or, again, one of our bishops, say, sends forth a letter condemning secret societies or issues a pastoral dealing with the new marriage laws—are we to say that these documents are intended to teach the whole way of salvation to all men, that they profess to state the whole Catholic creed? The question has only to be asked to expose its absurdity. Yet precisely the same question may be put about the position of Paul's epistles.

True, he was an apostle and consequently inspired, and his letters are the written Word of God and therefore are a final and decisive authority on the various points of which they treat, if properly understood, but that does not alter the fact that they nowhere claim to state the whole of Christian truth or to be a complete guide of salvation to anyone; they already presuppose the knowledge of the Christian faith among those to whom they are addressed; they are written to believers, not to unbelievers; in one word, the Church existed and did its work before they were written, and it would still have done so even though they had never been written at all. Paul's letters (for we are taking his merely as a sample of all) date from the year A.D. 52 to A.D. 68; Jesus Christ ascended to heaven leaving his Church to evangelize the world, A.D. 33; and we may confidently assert that the very last place we should expect to find a complete summary of Christian doctrine is in the epistles of the New Testament.

There is no need to delay further on the matter. I think I have made it clear enough how the various books of the New Testament took their origin. In so explaining the state of the case, we are not undervaluing the written Word of God or placing it on a level inferior to what it deserves. We are simply showing the position it was meant to occupy in the economy of the Christian Church. It was written by the Church, by members (apostles and evangelists) of the Church; it belongs to the Church, and it is her office, therefore, to declare what it means.

It is intended for instruction, meditation, spiritual reading, encouragement, devotion, and also serves as proof and testimony of the Church's doctrines and divine authority; but as a complete and exclusive guide to heaven in the hands of every man—this it never was and never could be. The Bible *in* the Church; the Church *before* the Bible—the Church the *maker* and *interpreter* of the Bible—that is right. The Bible above the Church; the Bible independent of the

Church; the Bible, and the Bible only, the religion of Christians—
that is wrong. The one is the Catholic position; the other is the
Protestant.

IV

The Church Compiles the New Testament

W E KNOW THAT THE GOSPELS and epistles of the New Testament were read aloud to the congregations of Christians that met on the first day of the week for Holy Mass (just as they are still among ourselves), one Gospel here, another there; one epistle of Paul in one place, another in another, all scattered about in various parts of the world where there were bodies of Christians. And the next question that naturally occurs to us is, When were these separate works gathered together so as to form a volume and added to the Old Testament to make up what we now call the Bible? Well, they were not collected for the best part of three hundred years.

Here again I am afraid is a hard nut for Protestants to crack. Though we admit that the separate works composing the New Testament were now in existence, yet they were for centuries not to be found altogether in one volume, were not obtainable by multitudes of Christians, and even were altogether unknown to many in different parts of the world. How then could they possibly form a guide to heaven and the chart of salvation for those who had never seen or read or known about them?

It is a fact of history that the Council of Carthage, which was held in A.D. 397, mainly through the influence of Augustine, settled the canon or collection of New Testament Scriptures as Catholics have them now and decreed that its decision should be sent on to Rome for confirmation. No council (that is, no gathering of the

17

bishops of the Catholic Church for the settlement of some point of doctrine) was ever considered to be authoritative or binding unless it was approved and confirmed by the Roman pontiff, while the decisions of every general council that has received the approval of Rome are binding on the consciences of all Catholics. The Council of Carthage, then, is the first known to us in which we find a clear and undisputed catalogue of all the New Testament books as we have them in Bibles now.

It is true that many Fathers, Doctors, and writers of the Church in the first three centuries from time to time mention by name many of the various Gospels and epistles, and some, as we come nearer 397, even refer to a collection already existing in places. For example, we find Constantine, the first Christian Emperor, after the Council of Nicaea applying to Eusebius, Bishop of Caesarea, and a great scholar, to provide fifty copies of the Christian Scriptures for public use in the churches of Constantinople, his new capital. This was in A.D. 332. The contents of these copies are known to us, perhaps (according to some, even probably) one of these very copies of Eusebius's handiwork has come down to us; but they are not precisely the same as our New Testament, though very nearly so.

Again, we find lists of the books of the New Testament drawn up by Athanasius, Jerome, Augustine, and many other great authorities, as witnessing to what was generally acknowledged as inspired Scripture in their day and generation and country, but I repeat that none of these corresponds perfectly to the collection in the Bible that we possess now; we must wait till 397 for the Council of Carthage before we find the complete collection of New Testament books settled as we have it today and as all Christendom had it till the sixteenth century, when the Reformers changed it.

You may ask me, however, What was the difference between the lists of New Testament books found in various countries and different authors before 397 and the catalogue drawn up at the Council of that date? Well, that introduces us to a very important point which tells us eloquently of the office that the Catholic Church performed, under God the Holy Ghost, in selecting and sifting and stamping with her divine authority the Scriptures of the

New Law, and I make bold to say that a calm consideration of the part that Rome took in the making and drawing up and preserving of the Christian Scriptures will convince any impartial mind that to the Catholic Church alone, so much maligned, we owe it that we know what the New Testament should consist of and why precisely it consists of these books and of no others and that without her we should, humanly speaking, have had no New Testament at all or, if a New Testament, then one in which works spurious and works genuine would have been mixed up in ruinous and inextricable confusion.

I have used the words "spurious" and "genuine" in regard to the Gospels and epistles in the Christian Church. You are horrified and hold up your hands and exclaim: "Lord, save us! Here we have a higher critic and a Modernist." Not at all, dear reader; quite the reverse, I assure you. Observe, I have said in "the Christian Church" —I did not say "in the Bible," for there is nothing spurious in the Bible. But why? Simply because the Roman See in the fourth century of our era prevented anything spurious being admitted into it.

There were spurious books floating about "in the Christian Church" without a doubt in the early centuries; this is certain, because we know their very names; and it is precisely in her rejection of these, and in her guarding the collection of inspired writings from being mixed up with them, that we shall now see the great work that the Catholic Church did, under God's Holy Spirit, for all succeeding generations of Christians, whether within the fold or outside of it. It is through the Roman Catholic Church that Protestants have got their Bible; there is not (to paraphrase some words of Newman) a Protestant that vilifies and condemns the Catholic Church for her treatment of Holy Scripture, but owes it to that Church that he has the Scripture at all.

What Almighty God might have done if Rome had not handed down the Bible to us is a fruitless speculation with which we have nothing whatever to do. It is a contingent possibility belonging to an order of things which has never existed, except in imagination. What we are concerned with is the order of things and the sequence of history in which we are now living and which we know and which consequently God has divinely disposed, and in this providential arrangement of history it is a fact, as clear as any other historical fact, that Almighty God chose the Catholic Church, and her only, to give us his Holy Scriptures and to give us them as we have them now, neither greater nor less. This I shall now proceed to prove.

1. Before the collection of New Testament books was finally settled at the Council of Carthage, 397, we find that there were three distinct classes into which the Christian writings were divided. This we know (and every scholar admits it) from the works of early Christian writers like Eusebius, Jerome, Epiphanius, and a whole host of others that we could name. These classes were the books "acknowledged" as canonical, books "disputed" or "controverted," books declared "spurious" or false.

In the first class those acknowledged by Christians everywhere to be genuine and authentic and to have been written by apostolic men, we find such books as the four Gospels, thirteen epistles of Paul, Acts of the Apostles. These were recognized East and West as "canonical," genuinely the works of the apostles and evangelists whose names they bore, worthy of being in the "canon" or sacred collection of inspired writings of the Church, and read aloud at Holy Mass.

But there was a second class—and Protestants should particularly take notice of the fact, as it utterly undermines their rule of faith, "the Bible and the Bible only"—of books that were disputed, controverted, in some places acknowledged, in others rejected; among these we actually find the Epistle of James, Epistle of Jude, Second Epistle of Peter; Second and Third of John, Epistle to the Hebrews, and the Apocalypse of John. There were doubts about these works; perhaps, it was said, they were not really written by apostles, or apostolic men, or by the men whose names they carried; in some parts of the Christian world they were suspected, though in others unhesitatingly received as genuine. There is no getting out of this fact, then: Some of the books of our Bible which we, Catholic and Protestant alike, now recognize as inspired and as the written Word of God, were at one time, indeed for long years, viewed with suspicion, doubted, disputed, as not possessing the same authority as the others. (I am speaking only of the New Testament books; the same could be proved, if there were space, of the Old Testament, but the New Testament suffices abundantly for the argument.)

But further still—what is even more striking and is equally fatal to the Protestant theory—in this second class of "controverted" and doubtful books some were to be found which are not now in our New Testament at all, but which were by many considered to be inspired and apostolic, or were actually read at the public worship of the Christians, or were used for instructions to the newly converted; in short, ranked in some places as equal to the works of James or Peter or Jude.

Among these we may mention specially the "Shepherd" of Hermas, the Epistle of Barnabas, the Doctrine of the Twelve Apostles, Apostolic Constitutions, Gospel According to the Hebrews, Paul's Epistle to the Laodiceans, Epistle of Clement, and others. Why are these not in our Bible today? We shall see in a minute.

Lastly there was a third class of books, floating about before 397, which were never acknowledged as of any value in the Church, nor treated as having apostolic authority, seeing that they were obviously spurious and false, full of absurd fables, superstitions, puerilities, and stories and miracles of our Lord and his apostles which made them a laughingstock to the world. Of these some have survived, and we have them today, to let us see what stamp of writing they were; most have perished. But we know the names of about fifty Gospels (such as the Gospel of James, the Gospel of Thomas, and the like), about twenty-two Acts (like the Acts of Pilate, Acts of Paul and Thecla, and others), and a smaller number of epistles and apocalypses. These were condemned and rejected wholesale as "Apocrypha"—that is, false, spurious, uncanonical.

2. This then being the state of matters, you can see at once what perplexity arose for the poor Christians in days of persecution, when they were required to surrender their sacred books. The Emperor Diocletian, for example, who inaugurated a terrible war against the Christians, issued an edict in 303 that all the churches should be razed to the ground and the Sacred Scriptures should be

delivered up to the pagan authorities to be burned. Well, the question was What was Sacred Scripture? If a Christian gave up an inspired writing to the pagans to save his life, he thereby became an apostate: He denied his faith, he betrayed his Lord and God; he saved his life, indeed, but he lost his soul. Some did this and were called "*traditores*," traitors, betrayers, "deliverers up" (of the Scriptures). Most, however, preferred martyrdom and, refusing to surrender the inspired writings, suffered the death.

But it was a most perplexing and harrowing question they had to decide—what really was Sacred Scripture? I am not bound to go to the stake for refusing to give up some "spurious" Gospel or epistle. Could I, then, safely give up some of the "controverted" or disputed books, like the epistle of James, or the Hebrews, or the Shepherd of Hermas, or the Epistle of Barnabas, or of Clement? There is no need to be a martyr by mistake. So the stress of persecution had the effect of making still more urgent the necessity of deciding once and for all what was to form the New Testament. What, definitely and precisely, were to be the books for which a Christian would be bound to lay down his life on pain of losing his soul?

3. Here, as I said before, comes in the Council of Carthage, A.D. 397, confirming and approving the decrees of a previous council (Hippo, 393) declaring, for all time to come, what was the exact collection of sacred writings thenceforth to be reckoned, to the exclusion of all others, as the inspired Scripture of the New Testament. That collection is precisely that which Catholics possess at this day in their Douay Bible. That decree of Carthage was never changed. It was sent to Rome for confirmation. As I have already remarked, a council, even though not a general council of the whole Catholic Church, may yet have its decrees made binding on the whole Church by the approval and will of the pope.

A second Council of Carthage over which Augustine presided, in 419, renewed the decrees of the former one and declared that its act was to be notified to Boniface, Bishop of Rome, for the purpose of confirming it. From that date all doubt ceased as to what was and what was not "spurious," "genuine," or "doubtful" among the Christian writings then known. Rome had spoken. A council of the Roman Catholic Church had settled it. You might hear a voice here or there, in East or West, in subsequent times, raking up some old doubt or raising a question as to whether this or that book of the New Testament is really what it claims to be or should be where it is. But it is a voice in the wilderness.

Rome had fixed the "canon" of the New Testament. There are henceforward but two classes of books—inspired and not inspired. Within the covers of the New Testament all is inspired; all without, known or unknown, is uninspired. Under the guidance of the Holy Ghost the council declared "This is genuine, that is false"; "this is apostolic, that is not apostolic." She sifted, weighed, discussed, selected, rejected, and finally decided what was what. Here she rejected a writing that was once very popular and reckoned by many as inspired and was actually read as Scripture at public service; there, again, she accepted another that was very much disputed and viewed with suspicion and said: "This is to go into the New Testament." She had the evidence before her, she had tradition to help her, and above all she had the assistance of the Holy Spirit to enable her to come to a right conclusion on so momentous a matter. In fact, her conclusion was received by all Christendom until the sixteenth century, when, as we shall see, men arose rebelling against her decision and altering the sacred volume.

But, at all events in regard to the New Testament, the Reformers left the books as they found them, and today their Testament contains exactly the same books as ours, and what I wish to drive home, is that they got these books from Rome, that without the Roman Catholic Church they would not have got them, and that the decrees of Carthage, 397 and 419, when all Christianity was Roman Catholic—reaffirmed by the Council of Florence, 1442, under Pope Eugenius IV, and the Council of Trent, 1546—these decrees of the Roman Church and these only are the means and the channel and the authority which Almighty God has used to hand down to us his written Word. Who can deny it? The Church existed before the Bible, she made the Bible, she selected its books, and she preserved it. She handed it down; through her we know what is the

Word of God and what the word of man, and hence to try at this time of day, as many do, to overthrow the Church by means of this very Bible, and to put it above the Church, and to revile her for destroying it and corrupting it—what is this but to strike the mother that reared them, to curse the hand that fed them, to turn against their best friend and benefactor, and to repay with ingratitude and slander the very guide and protector who has led them to drink of the water out of the Savior's fountains?

V

Deficiencies of the Protestant Bible

THE POINT THAT WE have arrived at now, if you remember, is this: The Catholic Church, through her popes and councils, gathered together the separate books that Christians venerated which existed in different parts of the world; sifted the chaff from the wheat, the false from the genuine; decisively and finally formed a collection—i.e., drew up a list or catalogue of inspired and apostolic writings into which no other book should ever be admitted, and declared that these, and these only, were the Sacred Scriptures of the New Testament.

The authorities that were mainly responsible for thus settling and closing the "canon" of Holy Scripture were the Councils of Hippo and of Carthage in the fourth century, under the influence of Augustine (at the latter of which two legatees were present from the pope), and the Popes Innocent I in 405 and Gelasius in 494, both of whom issued lists of Sacred Scripture identical with that fixed by the Councils. From that date all through the centuries this was the Christian's Bible. The Church never admitted any other; at the Council of Florence in the fifteenth century, and the Council of Trent in the sixteenth, and the Council of the Vatican in the nineteenth, she renewed her anathemas against all who should deny or dispute this collection of books as the inspired word of God.

1. What follows from this is self-evident. The same authority which made and collected and preserved these books alone has the right to claim them as her own and to say what the meaning of them

is. The Church of Paul and Peter and James in the first century was the same Church as that of the Council of Carthage and of Augustine in the fourth, of the Council of Florence in the fifteenth, and the Vatican in the nineteenth—one and the same body—growing and developing, certainly, as every living thing must do, but still preserving its identity and remaining essentially the same body, as a man of eighty is the same person as he was at forty and the same person at forty as he was at two.

The Catholic Church of today may be compared to a man who has grown from infancy to youth and from youth to middle-age. Suppose a man wrote a letter setting forth certain statements, Whom would you naturally ask to tell what the meaning of these statements was? Surely the man that wrote it. The Church wrote the New Testament; she, and she alone, can tell us what the meaning of it is.

Again, the Catholic Church is like a person who was present at the side of our Blessed Lord when he walked and talked in Galilee and Judea. Suppose, for a moment, that that man was gifted with perpetual youth (this by the way is an illustration of W. H. Mallock's *Doctrine and Doctrinal Disruption*, chap. 11) and also with perfect memory, heard all the teaching and explanations of our Redeemer and of his apostles, and retained them; he would be an invaluable witness and authority to consult, surely, so as to discover exactly what was the doctrine of Jesus Christ and of the twelve.

Such undoubtedly is the Catholic Church: not an individual person, but a corporate personality who lived with, indeed was called into being by, our divine Savior; in whose hearing he uttered all his teaching; who listened to the apostles in their day and generation, repeating and expounding the Savior's doctrine; who, ever young and ever strong, has persisted and lived all through the centuries and continues even till our own day fresh and keen in memory as ever and able to assure us, without fear of forgetting, or mixing things up, or adding things out of his own head, what exactly our Blessed Lord said, and taught, and meant, and did.

Suppose, again, the man we are imagining had written down much of what he heard Christ and the apostles say, but had not fully reported all and was able to supplement what was lacking by personal explanations which he gave from his perfect memory: that, again, is a figure of the Catholic Church. She wrote down much, indeed, and most important parts of our Lord's teaching, and of the apostolic explanation of it in Scripture, but nevertheless she did not intend it to be a complete and exhaustive account, apart from her own explanation of it; and, as a matter of fact, she is able from her own perpetual memory to give fuller and clearer accounts, and to add some things that are either omitted from the written report, or are only hinted at, or partially recorded, or mentioned merely in passing.

Such is the Catholic Church in relation to her own book, the New Testament. It is hers because she wrote it by her first apostles and preserved it and guarded it all down the ages by her popes and bishops; nobody else has any right to it whatsoever, any more than a stranger has the right to come into your house and break open your desk and pilfer your private documents. Therefore, I say that for people to step in 1,500 years after the Catholic Church had had possession of the Bible and to pretend that it is theirs, and that they alone know what the meaning of it is, and that the Scriptures alone, without the voice of the Catholic Church explaining them, are intended by God to be the guide and rule of faith—this is an absurd and groundless claim.

Only those who are ignorant of the true history of the Sacred Scriptures—their origin, authorship, and preservation—could pretend that there is any logic or common sense in such a mode of acting. The absurdity is magnified when it is remembered that the Protestants did not appropriate the whole of the Catholic books, but actually cast out some from the collection, took what remained, and elevated these into a new "canon" or volume of Sacred Scripture, such as had never been seen or heard of before, from the first to the sixteenth century, in any church, either in heaven above, or on earth beneath, or in the waters under the earth! Let us make good this charge.

2. Open a Protestant Bible, and you will find there are seven complete books a-wanting—that is, seven books fewer than there

are in the Catholic Bible, and seven fewer than there were in every collection and catalogue of Holy Scripture from the fourth to the sixteenth century. Their names are Tobit, Baruch, Judith, Wisdom, Ecclesiasticus (Sirach), 1 Maccabees, 2 Maccabees, together with seven chapters of the Book of Esther and sixty-six verses of the third chapter of Daniel, commonly called "the Song of the Three Children," (Daniel 3:29–40, Douay version), and the thirteenth and fourteenth chapters of Daniel. These were deliberately cut out and the Bible bound up without them. The criticisms and remarks of Luther, Calvin, and the Swiss and German Reformers about these seven books of the Old Testament show to what depths of impiety those unhappy men had allowed themselves to fall when they broke away from the true Church.

Even in regard to the New Testament it required all the powers of resistance on the part of the more conservative Reformers to prevent Luther from flinging out the Epistle of James as unworthy to remain within the volume of Holy Scripture—"an epistle of straw" he called it, "with no character of the gospel in it." In the same way and almost to the same degree, he dishonored the Epistle of Jude, and the Epistle to the Hebrews, and the beautiful Revelation of John, declaring they were not on the same footing as the rest of the books and did not contain the same amount of gospel (i.e., *his* gospel).

The presumptuous way, indeed, in which Luther, among others, poured contempt and doubt upon some of the inspired writings which had been acknowledged and cherished and venerated for 1,000 or 1,200 years would be scarcely credible were it not that we have his very words in cold print, which cannot lie and may be read in his biography or be seen quoted in such books as Dr. West-cott's *The Bible in the Church*. Why did he impugn such books as we have mentioned? Because they did not suit his new doctrines and opinions. He had arrived at the principle of private judgment—of picking and choosing religious doctrines. Whenever any book, such as the book of Maccabees, taught a doctrine that was repugnant to his individual taste—as, for example, that "it is a holy and wholesome thought to pray for the dead that they may be loosed from sins" (2 Macc. 12:46)—well, so much the worse for the book; "throw it overboard," was his sentence, and overboard it went. It was the same with passages and texts in those books which Luther allowed to remain and pronounced to be worthy to find a place within the boards of the new Reformed Bible. In short, he not only cast out certain books, but he mutilated some that were left.

For example, not pleased with Paul's doctrine "we are justified by faith," and fearing lest good works (a popish superstition) might creep in, he added the word "only" after Paul's words, making the sentence run: "We are justified by faith only," and so it reads in Lutheran Bibles to this day. An action such as that must surely be reprobated by all Bible Christians. What surprises us is the audacity of the man that could coolly change by a stroke of the pen a fundamental doctrine of the apostle of God, Paul, who wrote, as all admitted, under the inspiration of the Holy Ghost.

But this was the outcome of the Protestant standpoint, individual judgment: no authority outside of oneself. However ignorant, however stupid, however unlettered, you may—indeed you are bound—to cut and carve out a Bible and a religion for yourself. No pope, no council, no church shall enlighten you or dictate or hand down the doctrines of Christ. The result we have seen is the corruption of God's Holy Word.

3. Yet, in spite of all reviling of the Roman Church, the Reformers were forced to accept from her those Sacred Scriptures which they retained in their collection. Whatever Bible they have today, disfigured as it is, was taken from us. Blind indeed must be the Evangelical Christian who cannot recognize in the old Catholic Bible the quarry from which he has hewn the Testament he loves and studies, but with what loss, at what a sacrifice, in what a mutilated and disfigured condition!

That the Reformers should appropriate unabridged the Bible of the Catholic Church (which was the only volume of God's Scripture ever known on earth), even for the purpose of elevating it into a false position—this we could have understood; what staggers us is their deliberate excision from that sacred volume of some of the inspired books which had God for their author and their no less deliberate alteration of some of the texts of those books that were suffered to remain. It is on consideration of such points as these that pious persons outside the Catholic fold would do well to ask themselves the questions: Which Christian body really loves and reveres the Scriptures most? Which has proved, by its actions, its love and veneration? Which seems most likely to incur the anathema, recorded by John, that God will send upon those who shall take away from the words of the Book of Life (Rev. 22:19)?

VI

The Originals and Their Disappearance

YOU MAY NATURALLY ENOUGH ask me: "But how do you know all this? Where has the Bible come from? Have you got the original writings that came from the hand of Moses, or Paul, or John?" No, none of it, not a scrap or a letter, but we know from history and tradition that these were the books they wrote, and they have been handed down to us in a most wonderful way.

What we have now is the printed Bible; before the invention of printing in 1450, the Bible existed only in handwriting—what we call manuscript—and we have in our possession now copies of the Bible in manuscript, which were made as early as the fourth century, and these copies, which you can see with your own eyes at this day, contain the books which the Catholic Bible contains today, and that is how we know we are right in receiving these books as Scripture, as genuinely the work of the apostles and evangelists. Why is it that we have not the originals written by John and Paul and the rest? Well, there are several reasons to account for the disappearance of the originals.

1. The persecutors of the Church for the first 300 years of Christianity destroyed everything Christian that they could lay their hands on. Over and over again, barbarous pagans burst in upon Christian cities, and villages, and churches, and burned all the sacred things they could find. And not only so, but they especially compelled Christians (as we saw before) to deliver up their sacred books, under pain of death, and then consigned them to the flames.

31

Among these, doubtless, some of the writings that came from the hand of the apostle and evangelist perished.

2. Again, we must remember, the material which the inspired authors used for writing their Gospels and epistles was very easily destroyed; it was perishable to a degree. It was called papyrus (I shall explain what it was made of in a moment), very frail and brittle, and not made to last to any great age; its delicate quality, no doubt, accounts for the loss of some of the choicest treasures of ancient literature, as well as of the original handwriting of the New Testament writers. We know of no manuscript of the New Testament existing now which is written on papyrus.

3. Furthermore, when in various churches throughout the first centuries copies were made of the inspired writings, there was not the same necessity for preserving the originals. The first Christians had no superstitious or idolatrous veneration for the Sacred Scriptures, such as seems to prevail among some people today; they did not consider it necessary for salvation that the very handwriting of Paul or Matthew should be preserved, inspired by God though these men were.

They had the living, infallible Church to teach and guide them by the mouth of her popes and bishops—and to teach them not only all that could be found in the Sacred Scriptures, but the true meaning of it as well, so that we need not be surprised that they were content with mere *copies* of the original works of the inspired writers.

So soon as a more beautiful or correct copy was made, an earlier and rougher one was simply allowed to perish. There is nothing strange or unusual in all this; it is just what holds good in the secular world. We do not doubt the terms or provisions of the Magna Carta because we have not seen the original; a copy, if we are sure it is correct, is good enough for us.

Well, then, the originals, as they came from the hand of apostle and evangelist, have totally disappeared. This is what infidels and skeptics taunt us with and cast in our teeth: "You cannot produce," they say, "the handwriting of those from whom you derive your religion, neither the Founder nor his apostles; your Gospels and epistles are a fraud; they were not written by these men at all, but are the invention of a later age, and consequently we cannot depend upon the contents of them or believe what they tell us about Jesus Christ." Of course, these attacks fall harmlessly upon us Catholics, because we do not profess to rest our religion upon the Bible alone, and are independent of it, and would be just as we are and what we are though there were no Bible at all. It is those who have staked their very existence upon that book, and must stand or fall with it, that are called upon to defend themselves against the critics.

But I shall only remark here that the argument of infidel and skeptic would, if logically applied, discredit not only the Bible, but many other books which they themselves accept and believe without hesitation. There is far more evidence for the Bible than there is for certain books of classical antiquity which no one dreams of disputing.

There are, for example, only fifteen manuscripts of the works of Herodotus, and none earlier than the tenth century A.D., yet he lived 400 years before Christ. The oldest manuscript of the works of Thucydides is of the eleventh century A.D., yet he flourished and wrote more than 400 years before Christ. Shall we say, then, "I want to see the handwriting of Thucydides and Herodotus, else I shall not believe these are their genuine works. You have no copy of their writings near the time they lived—none, indeed, till 1,400 years after them; they must be a fraud and a forgery"?

Scholars with no religion at all would say we were fit for an asylum if we took up that position, yet it would be a far more reasonable attitude than that which they take up toward the Bible. Why? Because there are known to have been many thousand copies of the Testament in existence by the third century—i.e., only a century or two after John—and we know for certain there are 3,000 existing at the present day, ranging from the fourth century downward.

The fact is, the wealth of evidence for the genuineness of the New Testament is simply stupendous, and, in comparison with many ancient histories which are received without question on the authority of late and few and bad copies, the sacred volume is founded on a rock. But let us pass on; enough for us to know that God has willed that the handiwork of every inspired writer, from Moses down to John, should have perished from among men and that he has entrusted our salvation to something more stable and enduring than a dead book or an indecipherable manuscript—the living and infallible Church of Christ: *Ubi Ecclesia, ibi Christus.*

Now I wish to devote what remains of this chapter to say something about the material instruments that were used for the writing and transmission of Holy Scriptures in the earliest days. A brief review of the materials employed, and the dangers of loss and of corruption which necessarily accompanied the work, will convince us more than ever of the absolute need of some divinely protected authority like the Catholic Church to guard the gospel from error and destruction and preserve "the apostolic deposit" (as it is called) from sharing the fate which is liable to overtake all things that are, as says Paul, contained in "earthen vessels."

Various materials were used in ancient times for writing, such as stone, pottery, bark of trees, leather, and clay tablets among the Babylonians and Egyptians.

1. But before Christianity, and for the first few ages of our era, *papyrus* was used, which has given its name to our "paper." It was formed of the bark of the reed or bulrush, which once grew plentifully on the Nile banks. First split into layers, it was then glued by overlapping the edges, and another layer glued to this at right angles to prevent splitting, and, after sizing and drying, it formed a suitable writing surface.

Thousands of rolls of papyrus have been found in Egyptian and Babylonian tombs and beneath the buried city of Herculaneum, owing their preservation probably to the very fact of being buried, because, as I said, the substance was very brittle, frail, and perishable and unsuited for rough usage. Though probably many copies of the Bible were originally written on this papyrus (and most likely the inspired writers used it themselves), none have survived the wreck of ages. It is this material John is referring to when he says to his correspondent in 2 John, verse 12: "Having more things to write to you, I would not by paper and ink."

2. When, in the course of time, papyrus fell into comparative disuse from its unsuitableness and fragility, the skins of animals came to be used. This material had two names; if it was made out of the skin of sheep or goats, it was called parchment; if made of the skin of delicate young calves, it was called *vellum*. Vellum was used in earlier days, but, being very dear and hard to obtain, gave place to a large extent to the coarser parchment. Paul speaks about this stuff when he tells Timothy (2 Tim. 4:13) to "bring the books, but especially the parchments."

Most of the New Testament manuscripts which we possess today are written on this material. A curious consequence of the costliness of this substance was this, that the same sheet of vellum was made to do duty twice over and became what is termed a palimpsest, which means "rubbed again." A scribe, say, of the tenth century, unable to purchase a new supply of vellum, would take a sheet containing, perhaps, a writing of the second century, which had become worn out through age and difficult to decipher; he would wash or scrape out the old ink and use the surface over again for copying out some other work in which the living generation felt more interest.

It goes without saying that in many cases the writing thus blotted out was of far greater value than that which replaced it; indeed, some of the most precious monuments of sacred learning are of this description, and they were discovered in this way. The process of erasing or sponging out the ancient ink was seldom so perfectly done as to prevent all traces of it still remaining, and some strokes of the older hand might often be seen peeping out beneath the more modern writing. In 1834 some chemical mixture was discovered which was applied with much success and had the effect of restoring the faded lines and letters of those venerable records.

Cardinal Mai, a man of colossal scholarship and untiring industry and a member of the Sacred College in Rome under Pope Gregory XVI, was a perfect expert in this branch of research and, by his ceaseless labors and ferret-like hunts in the Vatican library, brought to light some remarkable old manuscripts and some priceless works of antiquity. Among these, all students have to thank him for restoring a long lost work of Cicero (*De Republicâ*) that was known to have existed previously and which the Cardinal unearthed from beneath Augustine's *Commentary on the Psalms*!

The most important manuscript of the New Testament of this description is called the Codex of Ephraem. About 200 years ago it was noticed that this curious-looking vellum, all soiled and stained, and hitherto thought to contain only the theological discourses of Ephraem, an old Syrian Father, was showing dim traces and faint lines of some older writing beneath. The chemical mixture was applied, and lo! what should appear but a most ancient and valuable copy of Holy Scriptures of handwriting not later than the fifth century! This had been coolly scrubbed out by some impecunious scribe of the twelfth century to make room for his favorite work, the discourses of Ephraem!

Let us charitably hope that the good monk (as he probably was) did not know what he was scrubbing out. At all events, it was brought into France by Queen Catherine de Medici and is now safely preserved in the Royal Library at Paris, containing on the same page two works, one written on top of the other with a period of 700 years between them.

I have told you about the sheets used by the earliest writers of the New Testament: What kind of pen and ink had they?

1. Well, for the brittle papyrus, a reed was used, much the same as that still in use in the East, but of course for writing on hard tough parchment or vellum a metal pen, or stylus, was required. It is to this John refers in his third epistle (verse 13) when he says, "I had many things to write unto thee, but I would not by ink and pen write to thee." The strokes of these pens may still be seen quite clearly impressed on the parchment, even though all trace of the ink has utterly vanished.

Besides this, a bodkin or needle was employed, by means of which, along with a ruler, a blank leaf or sheet was carefully divided into columns and lines; and on nearly all the manuscripts these lines and marks may still be seen, sometimes so firmly and deeply drawn that those on one side of the leaf have penetrated through to the other side, without, however, cutting the vellum.

2. The ink used was a composition of soot or lampblack or burnt shavings of ivory, mixed with gum or wine-lees or alum (for all these elements entered into it). In most ancient manuscripts, unfortunately, the ink has for the most part turned red or brown, or become very pale, or peeled off, or eaten through the vellum, and in many cases later hands have ruthlessly retraced the ancient letters, making the original writing look much coarser. But we know that many colored inks were used, such as red, green, blue, or purple, and they are often quite brilliant to this day.

3. As to the shape of the manuscripts, the oldest form was that of a roll. They were generally fixed on two rollers, so that the part read (for example in public worship) could be wound out of sight and a new portion brought to view. This was the kind of thing that was handed to our Lord when he went into the synagogue at Nazareth on the Sabbath. "He unfolded the book," and read, and then, "when he had folded the book, he restored it to the minister" (Luke 4:17–20). When not in use these rolls were kept in round boxes or cylinders and sometimes in cases of silver or cloth of great value.

The leaves of parchment were sometimes of considerable size, such as folio, but generally the shape was what we know as quarto or small folio, and some were octavo. The skin of one animal, especially if an antelope, could furnish many sheets of parchment; but if the animal was a small calf, then its skin could only furnish very few sheets; an instance of this is the manuscript called the Sinaitic (now in St. Petersburg) whose sheets are so large that the skin of a single animal (believed to have been the youngest and finest antelope) could only provide two sheets (eight pages).

4. The page was divided into two or three or four columns (though the latter is very rare). The writing was of two distinct kinds, one called uncial (meaning an inch), consisting entirely of capital letters, with no connection between the letters and no space between words at all; the other style, which is later, was cursive (that is, a running hand) like our ordinary handwriting, with capitals only at the beginning of sentences, and in this case the letters are joined together and there is a space between words. The uncial style (consisting of capitals only) was prevalent for the first three

centuries of our era; in the fourth century the cursive began and continued till the invention of printing.

5. Originally, I need hardly say, there was no such thing in the manuscripts as divisions into chapters and verses, and no points or full stops or commas, to let you know where one sentence began and the next finished—hence the reading of one of these ancient records is a matter of some difficulty to the unscholarly. The division into chapters so familiar to us in our modern Bibles was the invention either of Cardinal Hugo, a Dominican, in 1248 or more probably of Stephen Langton, Archbishop of Canterbury (d. 1227); it is no calumny upon the reputation of either of these great men to say that the division is not very satisfactory. He is not happy in his method of splitting up the page of Scripture; the chapters are of very unequal length and frequently interrupt a narrative or argument or an incident in an inconvenient way, as anyone may see for himself by looking up such passages as Acts 21:40 or Acts 4 and 5 or 1 Corinthians 12 and 13.

The division again into verses was the work of one Robert Stephens, and the first English version in which it appeared was the Geneva Bible, 1560. This gentleman seems to have completed his performance on a journey between Paris and Lyons (*inter equitandum*, as the Latin biographer phrases it), probably while stopping overnights in inns and hostels. "I think," an old commentator quaintly remarks, "it had been better done on his knees in the closet." To this I would venture to add that his achievement must share the same criticism of inappropriateness as the arrangement into chapters.

6. The manuscripts of the Bible, as I before remarked, now known to be in existence number about 3,000, of which the vast majority are in running hand and hence are subsequent to the fourth century. There are none of course later than the sixteenth century, for then the book began to be printed, and none have yet been found earlier than the fourth. Their age, the precise century in which they were written, it is not always easy to determine.

About the tenth century the scribes who copied them began to notify the date in a corner of the page, but before that time we can only judge by various characteristics that appear in the manuscripts. For example, the more simple and upright and regular the letters are, the less flourish and ornamentation they have about them, the nearer equality there is between the height and breadth of the characters—the more ancient we may be sure is the manuscript. Then, of course, we can often tell the age of a manuscript approximately at least by the kind of pictures the scribe had painted in it, the illustrations he had introduced, and the ornamenting of the first letter of a sentence or on the top of a page, for we know in what century that particular style of illumination prevailed.

It would be impossible to give anyone who had never seen any specimens of these wonderful old manuscripts a proper idea of their appearance or make him realize their unique beauty. There they are today, perfect marvels of human skill and workmanship; manuscripts of every kind; old parchments all stained and worn; books of faded purple lettered with silver and their pages beautifully designed and ornamented; bundles of finest vellum, yellow with age and bright even yet with the gold and vermilion laid on by pious hands 1,000 years ago—in many shapes, in many colors, in many languages.

There they are, scattered throughout the libraries and museums of Europe, challenging the admiration of everyone that beholds them for the astonishing beauty, clearness, and regularity of their lettering and the incomparable illumination of their capitals and headings—still at this day, after so many centuries of change and chance, charming the eye of all with their soft yet brilliant colors and defying our modern scribes to produce anything the least approaching them in loveliness. There lie the sacred records, hoary with age, fragile, slender, timeworn, bearing upon their front clear proofs of their ancient birth; yet with the bloom of youth still clinging about them.

We simply stand and wonder, and we also despair. We speak glibly of the "Dark Ages" and despise their monks and friars (and I shall, with your leave, speak a little more about them immediately), but one thing at least is certain, and that is that not in the wide world today could any of their critics find a craftsman to make a copy of Holy Scripture worthy to be compared for beauty, clearness, and finish with any one of the hundreds of copies produced in the convents and monasteries of medieval Europe.

VII

Variations in Text Fatal to Protestant Theory

I HAVE MENTIONED MONASTERIES, and justly so, for there is no doubt that the vast majority, indeed practically all of these venerable pages were traced by the hand of some ecclesiastic. The clergy were the only persons who had learning enough for it. What care, what zeal, what loving labor was spent by these holy men in their work of transcribing the word of Scripture we can judge by viewing their handiwork. Yet the work was necessarily very slow and liable to error, and that errors did creep in we know from the simple fact that there are about 200,000 variations in the text of the Bible as written in these manuscripts that we have today. This is not to be wondered at, if you remember that there are 35,000 verses in the Bible.

Consider the various ways in which corruptions and variations could be introduced. The variations might have been intentionally or unintentionally introduced.

1. Under the first class we unfortunately must reckon those changes which were made by heretics to suit their particular doctrine or practice, just as, for example, the Lutherans added the word "only" to Paul's words to fit in with their newfangled notion about "justification by faith only." Or again, a scribe might really think that he was improving the old copy from which he was transcribing by putting in a word here or leaving out a word there, or putting in a different word, so as to make the sentence clearer or the sense better.

41

2. It is satisfactory to be assured (as we are) that the vast majority of changes and varieties of readings in these old manuscripts is entirely due to some unintentional cause. The scribe might be tired or sleepy or exhausted with much writing, and might easily skip over a word or indeed a whole sentence, or miss a line or repeat a line, or make a mistake when he came to the end of a line or a sentence; he might be interrupted in his work and begin at the wrong word when he recommenced.

Or he might have bad eyesight (some lost it altogether through copying so much); or not know really what was the proper division to make of the words he was copying, especially if the copy he was busy with was one of the old uncials, with no stops and no pauses and no division between words or sentences; or he might, if he were writing at the dictation of another, not hear very well, or pick up a word or phrase wrongly, as, for example, the woman did when she wrote "Satan died here" for a milliner's shop, instead of "Satin dyed here."

Or he might actually embody and copy into the sacred text of the Gospels words or notes or phrases which did not really belong to the Gospel at all, but had been written on the margin of the parchment by some previous scribe merely to explain things. These "glosses," as they are called, undoubtedly have crept in to some copies, and the Protestants are guilty of repeating one every time they say their form of the Lord's Prayer, with its ending "For thine is the kingdom and the power and the glory forever. Amen." Such an addition was not uttered by our Lord; Catholics consequently do not use it.

These are some (and not all) of the ways in which you could easily see that differences could arise in the various copies made by old scribes. Put six men today to report a speech by any orator; there will be considerable variety in their reports, as one can prove by comparing different newspaper accounts of the same speech any morning.

I do not say that the differences will always signify much or substantially alter the speaker's meaning, yet there they are, and sometimes they may be serious enough; if these things happen daily, even now with all our advanced and highly developed methods of printing, how much more would they happen in the old days before printing, when hand and brain and eyesight and hearing could make so many blunders? One single letter changed would conceivably reverse the meaning of the whole sentence.

I shall not alarm you by flaunting specimens from the Greek or Hebrew, but shall make plain enough what I mean by recording an instance occurring in our own days in our own tongue. An old provost of a certain East Lothian town had died and been duly buried, and a headstone had been erected bearing the fitting inscription from Paul's First Epistle to the Corinthians (15:52): "And we shall be changed." It was finished on the Saturday, but a deed of darkness was done before the "Sabbath" morning. The minister had a son who loved a practical joke. He got accomplices for his shameful deed; they hoisted him up, and in cold blood he took putty and obliterated the letter "c" in "changed." On the "Sabbath" the godly, passing around, with long faces, Bibles, and white handkerchiefs, to view the old provost's tombstone, learned for the first time that the apostle taught "And we shall be hanged."

You see what I mean? Well, the Bibles, before printing, are full of varieties and differences and blunders. Which of them all is correct? Pious Protestants may hold up their hands in horror and cry out, "There are no mistakes in the Bible! It is all inspired! It is God's own book!" Quite true, if you get God's own book, the originals as they came from the hand of apostle, prophet, and evangelist. These, and these men only, were inspired and protected from making mistakes. God never promised that every individual scribe (perhaps sleepy-headed, or stupid, or heretical) who took in hand the copying out of the New Testament would be infallibly secure from committing errors in his work.

The original Scripture is free from error because it has God for its author; so teaches the Catholic Church; and the Catholic Bible, too, the Vulgate, is a correct version of the Scripture; but that does not alter the fact that there are scores, nay thousands, of differences in the old manuscripts and copies of the Bible that were written before the days of printing; I should like any inquiring Protestants to ponder over this fact and see how they can possibly reconcile it with their principle that the Bible alone is the all-sufficient guide to salvation. Which Bible? Are you sure you have got the right Bible? Are you certain that your Bible contains exactly the words, and all the words, and only the words, that came from the hands of apostle and evangelist? Are you sure that no other words have crept in or that none have been dropped out? Can you study the Hebrew and Greek and Latin manuscripts and versions, page by page, and compare them, and compile for yourself a copy of Holy Scripture identical with that written by the inspired authors from Moses to John? If you cannot—and you see at once that it is impossible—then do not talk about "the Bible and the Bible only."

You know perfectly well that you must trust to some authority outside of yourself to give you the Bible. The Bible you are using today was handed down to you. You have, in fact, allowed some third party to come between you and God, a thing quite repugnant to the Protestant theory.

We Catholics, on the other hand, glory in having some third party to come between us and God, because God himself has given it to us, namely, the Catholic Church, to teach us and lead us to him. We believe in the Bible interpreted for us by that Church, because God entrusted to her the Bible as part of his word, and gave her a promise that she would never err in telling us what it means and explaining to us the "many things hard to be understood," which Peter tells us are to be found within it. Though there were as many million variations as there are thousands in the different copies of the Bible, we should be still unmoved, for we have a "Teacher sent from God," above and independent of all Scripture, who, assisted by the Holy Ghost, speaks with divine authority, and whose voice to us is the voice of God.

It matters not to us when a Christian may have lived on earth; whether before any of the New Testament was written at all, or before it was collected, into one volume, or before it was printed, or after it has been printed; no matter to us whether there are 1,000 or 1,000,000 variations in texts and passages and chapters of ancient copies of which our modern Bibles are compiled; we do not hazard our salvation on such a precarious and unreliable support. We rather take that Guide who is "yesterday and today and the same for ever," and who speaks to us with a living voice, and who can never make a mistake; who is never uncertain or doubtful or wavering in her utterances, never denying today what she affirmed yesterday, but ever clear, definite, dogmatic; enlightening what is dark and making plain what is obscure to the minds of men.

This is the Catholic Church, established by Almighty God as his organ and mouthpiece and interpreter, unaffected by the changes and unshaken by the discoveries of ages. To her we listen; her we obey; to her we submit our judgment and our intellect, knowing she will never lead us wrong. In her we find peace and comfort, satisfaction and solution of all our difficulties, for she is the one infallible teacher and guide appointed by God. This is a logical, consistent, clear, and intelligible method of attaining and preserving the truth, a perfect plan and scheme of Christianity. It is the Catholic plan; it is Christ's plan. What plan have any others to substitute for it that can stand a moment's analysis at the bar of reason, history, common sense, or even of Holy Scripture itself?

VIII

Our Debt to the Monks

THUS FAR WE HAVE BEEN SPEAKING of the Bible as found written in the old manuscripts, mostly in the very early centuries of Christianity. The next question, after settling how the Bible was made and collected and committed to writing, is, How was it preserved and multiplied and diffused throughout the centuries previous to the invention of printing? You will bear in mind that we are as yet a long way off from the day when the first printing press was invented or set up. Did the people at large know anything at all about the Sacred Scriptures before they were printed and put into their hands?

Here we are suddenly plunged into the Middle Ages; what was the history of the Holy Book during that time which people in these countries generally call "Dark"? If you have patience with me for a little while I shall prove to you that, just as the Catholic Church at the very beginning wrote and collected together the sacred books of the New Testament, so by her monks and friars and clergy generally she preserved them from destruction during the Middle Ages and made the people familiar with them and, in short, that it is to the Roman Church again under God that we owe the possession of the Bible in its integrity at the present day.

This will sound strange and startling in the ears of those who have imbibed the common notions about the Middle Ages. As I said, there was a traditional Protestant delusion about the Catholic Church and the Bible in general, so there is a traditional opinion which every good Protestant must adopt about those Ages of Faith, as we Catholics prefer to call them. The general idea is that they were centuries (from the eighth century to the end of the fourteenth) of profound ignorance, oppression, superstition, and universal misery—that the monks were debauched, greedy, and lazy—that the people in consequence were illiterate and immoral, only half civilized, and always fighting—that the whole of Europe was sunk in barbarism and darkness, men's intellects enslaved and their wills enervated, and all their natural energies paralyzed and benumbed by the blighting yoke of Rome—that (in the comprehensive language of the *Church of England Homilies*) "laity and clergy, learned and unlearned, all ages, sects, and degrees of men, women and children, of whole Christendom, had been altogether drowned in damnable idolatry, and that by the space of 800 years and more."

That is fairly sweeping. How they can reconcile that alleged state of things with the unconditioned promises of our Blessed Lord that "the gates of hell should never prevail against the Church," that he would "be with her always to the end of the world," and that the "Holy Ghost would lead them into all the truth" is to me a mystery. But let that pass. We are asked then to believe that during the Middle Ages true Christianity was overlaid and buried beneath a mass of popish fables and traditions and that of course the Bible in consequence was unknown except to a very few, was neglected and ignored and kept out of sight because it would have destroyed popery if it had been known. Only when the light of the Reformation shone out did the Holy Book appear openly in the world and become familiar to the faithful of Christ as that which was to "make them wise unto salvation."

I am not going to enter into a general defense of the condition of things in the Catholic world during these Ages of Faith, though, if time permitted, nothing would be more congenial to me. I would merely remark in passing that perhaps men of the twenty-first or twenty-second century will take the very same view of this age of ours as some people do now of the Middle Ages and will look back with horror upon it as a time when the world was desolated by famine, pestilence, and war, when nations of the earth amassed huge armies and built immense navies to slaughter each other and plunder each other's territories, when the condition of the poor was harsher and crueler than ever before in the history of the world since Christ was born, when there were on the one side some hundreds or thousands of capitalists, with some millionaires among them and, on the other, many millions of the laboring classes in deepest want and misery; multitudes on the very verge of starvation, wondering how they were to keep a roof over their heads or get a bit of food for themselves and for their children.

People in ages to come may regard this century with its boasted progress and civilization, and this land with 350 years of Protestantism behind it, as an age and a country where drunkenness and dishonesty and immorality and matrimonial unfaithfulness and extravagance and unbelief and youthful excesses and insubordination and barbarity of manners were so universally and so deeply rooted that the authorities of the kingdom were simply helpless to cope with them.

I am one of those who hold that the "Dark Ages" were ages full of light in comparison to these in which we are now living. The ages which built the gorgeous cathedrals and abbeys, whose ruins still stand as silent but eloquent witnesses of their past glory and beauty and still delight the eye and captivate the admiration of even the most unsympathetic beholder—those ages could not at least have been sunk in ignorance of architecture, or been insensible to the beautiful and the artistic, or been niggardly or ungenerous in their estimate of what was a worthy temple for the majesty of the God of heaven and earth and a dwelling-place fitting for the Lord of Hosts.

Again, the ages which covered the face of Europe with universities and schools of learning, which produced philosophers and theologians such as Thomas Aquinas and Bonaventure and Albertus Magnus and Scotus and Bacon, and which built up the scholastic system—a system which, for logical acuteness and metaphysical accuracy, for subtlety and unity and complete consistency, has never been equaled and which still stands unshaken by all attacks and triumphing over all its rivals that "have their day and cease to be" —that age could hardly have been intellectually dark or barren.

Once more: An age which produced saints like Dominic and Francis and Bernard and was fruitful in bringing forth orders of men and women for assisting our poor humanity in every form and stage of its existence—teaching the ignorant, caring for the sick and the afflicted, and even redeeming captives from the yoke of slavery —the age which witnessed the Crusades, those magnificent outbursts of Christian chivalry and of loyalty to Jesus Christ our Lord—when men, kings, princes, and subjects, seizing the Crusader's cross, went cheerfully to lay down their lives in myriads on the burning plains of Syria in their glorious attempts to rescue the Holy Sepulcher from the hand of Turk and infidel—that age, I say, cannot have been altogether devoid of the love of him who himself gave his life for men and whose feet had trod those sacred places in the days of his flesh.

People speak glibly nowadays of the ignorance of these far-back times, but it seems to me that no man who is really grounded in the truth of Christianity, who knows his *Pater Noster*, *Ave*, Creed, the Ten Commandments, and the seven sacraments and puts them into practice, can ever be said to be truly ignorant. He might not have been able to build a motor car or even to drive one, to turn out a steamship or a flying machine or speak the weird language of Esperanto. Neither could Peter or Joseph, for the matter of that.

Nevertheless the practical teaching the people of those ages received from priest and monk in church and school was, I submit, of far more real moral and intellectual value than the hash of scraps of hygiene and science, French and cookery, civics and art which is crammed into the unwilling brains of our twentieth-century public school children. Generally speaking, the medievalists, so despised, had the knowledge of God and of the world to come, and that was really the best knowledge they could have. (See the preface to Dr. Maitland's *Dark Ages*.)

But I am afraid I have been guilty of a serious digression; what we must do now is to confine ourselves to the single point as to how the Scriptures were preserved and multiplied and made known to the people in the Middle Ages. I shall first prove that the Bible was multiplied and preserved by the monks and priests. All must now admit that it was really in monasteries that multitudes of copies of the Holy Scriptures were made. Monasteries were centers of learning in those times even more than they are today, because education was not so widely spread. An indispensable part of the outfit of every monastery was a library. "A monastery without a library," writes a monk of the twelfth century to another monk, "is like a castle without an armory." He goes on to declare that the great defense in the monastic armory should be the Bible. Sometimes the libraries were very large, and we read of emperors and other great people borrowing from them.

The monks were the most learned men of those days and were by profession scholars, men who had renounced worldly pursuits and pleasures and dedicated themselves to a retired life of prayer and study, and one of the principal parts of their scholastic activity was the copying and transcribing of the Sacred Scriptures. For this purpose there was a large room called the *scriptorium*, in which a dozen or more monks could be engaged at one time, but there were also many monks employed, each in his own cell, which contained all the necessary apparatus for literary work. These cells were so arranged around the central heating chamber that in winter their hands would not get benumbed with so much writing.

Day by day, year after year, the monks would persevere in their holy labors, copying with loving care every letter of the sacred text from some old manuscript of the Bible, adorning and illuminating the pages of vellum with pictures and illustrations in purple and gold and silver coloring, so producing real works of art that excite the envy and admiration of modern generations. Some bishops and abbots wrote out with their own hands the whole of both the Old and the New Testaments for the use of their churches and monasteries. Even nuns—and this point I would bring under special notice—took their share in this pious and highly skilled labor. We read of one who copied with her own hands two whole Bibles and besides made six copies of several large portions of the Gospels and epistles.

Every monastery and church possessed at least one and some possessed many copies of the Bible and the Gospels. In those ages it was a common thing to copy out particular parts of the Bible (as well as the whole Bible)—for example, the Gospels, or the psalms, or epistles—so that many who could not afford to purchase a complete Bible were able to possess themselves of at least some part which was specially interesting or popular. This custom is truly Catholic, as it flourishes among us today.

At the end of our prayer books, for instance, we have Gospels and epistles for the Sundays, and various publishers, too, have issued the four Gospels separately, each by itself, and the practice seems to me to harmonize entirely with the very idea and structure of the Bible, which was originally composed of separate and independent portions, in use in different churches throughout Christendom. So we find that the monks and clergy often confined their work to copying out certain special portions of Sacred Scripture, and naturally the Gospels were the favorite part.

The work, we must remember, was very slow and expensive. Dr. Maitland reckons that it would require ten months for a scribe of those days to copy out a Bible and that £60 or £70 would have been required if he had been paid at the rate that law-stationers pay their writers. Of course, with the monks it was a labor of love and not for money; but this calculation of Dr. Maitland only refers to the work of copying; it leaves out of account the materials that had to be used, pen and ink and parchment.

Another authority (Buckingham) has made a more detailed calculation. Assuming that 427 skins of parchment would have been needed for the 35,000 verses, running into 127,000 folios, he reckons that a complete copy of Old and New Testaments could not have been purchased for less than £218. Yet Protestants stare in astonishment when you tell them that not everybody could sit by his fireside in those days with a Bible on his knees! Some princes (among them, I think, Charlemagne) gave the monks permission to hunt for deer in the royal forests, so as to get skins to make into parchment for copying work. I have no space to give elaborate proof of my assertion that, as a matter of course, all monasteries and churches possessed copies of the Scriptures in the Middle Ages. It stands to reason that those who made the copies would keep at least one for their own use in the monastery and another for the public services in the church. We read of one convent in Italy which had not money enough for the bare necessaries of life, yet managed to scrape up £50 to purchase a Bible.

Dr. Maitland, in his most valuable book *The Dark Ages*—he was a Protestant, librarian to the archbishop of Canterbury, a great student, and a most impartial scholar—gives page after page of instances, that came under his own notice in his researches, of religious houses that had Bibles and Testaments in their possession. Of course these are but casual specimens; the thing was so common that there was no need to chronicle the fact any more than you would chronicle the fact that A or B had a clock in his parlor in the nineteenth century. Kings and princes and popes often presented beautiful copies of the Bible to abbots and priors for use in their monastery, sometimes gloriously embellished within with painting and illuminations, written in letters of gold and silver, and bound in golden casing set with gems. We frequently read of such gifts. Not only the Bible, but other books used in the service of the Church, such as copies of the missal or psalter or Gospels, all containing great portions of Holy Scripture, were often presented as gifts by great personages in Church or state, bound in gold or ivory or silver of the utmost purity and marvelously adorned and studded with pearls and precious stones. Nothing was considered too costly or too magnificent to lavish on the sacred volume.

But I suppose that when we find popes like Leo III and Leo IV, and emperors like Henry II and Lewis the Debonair, and bishops like Hincmar of Rheims and Ralph of Rochester, and dukes like Hugh of Burgundy, and numberless abbots and priors in the eighth and ninth centuries causing copies of the Sacred Scriptures to be made and gifted to monasteries and churches throughout Europe, this must be taken as evidence of Rome's hatred of the Word of God and her fear of its becoming known or read or studied! Yet that this was the common custom for hundreds of years is a fact of history that is quite beyond the region of doubt. Moreover, the

Sacred Scriptures were a favorite subject of study among the clergy, and a popular occupation was the writing of commentaries upon them, as all priests at least are aware, from having to recite portions of them every day, ranging from the age of Leo the Great and Gregory down to Bernard and Anselm.

One could go on at any length accumulating evidence as to the fact of monks and priests reproducing and transmitting copies of the Bible from century to century, before the days of Wycliff and Luther, but there is no need, because I am not writing a treatise on the subject, but merely adducing a few proofs of my assertions and trying to show how utterly absurd is the contention that Rome hates the Bible and did her best to keep it a locked and sealed book and even to destroy it throughout the Middle Ages.

Surely nothing but the crassest ignorance or the blindest prejudice could support a theory so flatly contradicted by the simplest facts of history. The real truth of the matter is that it is the Middle Ages which have been a closed and sealed book to Protestants and that only now, owing to the honest and patient research of impartial scholars among them, are the treasures of those grand centuries being unlocked and brought to their view.

It is this ignorance or prejudice which explains to me a feature that would be otherwise unaccountable in the histories of the Bible written by non-Catholics. I have consulted many of them, and they all, with hardly an exception, either skip over this period of the Bible's existence altogether or dismiss it with a few offhand references. They jump right over from the inspired writers themselves, or perhaps from the fourth century, when the canon was fixed, to John Wycliff, "The Morning Star of the Reformation," leaving blank the intermediate centuries, plunged, as they imagine, in worse than Egyptian darkness.

But I ask, Is this fair or honest? Is it consistent with a love of truth thus to suppress the fact, which is now happily beginning to dawn on the more enlightened minds, that it was the monks and clergy of the Catholic Church who, during all these ages, preserved, multiplied, and perpetuated the Sacred Scriptures? The Bible on its human side is a perishable article. Inspired by God though it be, it was yet, by the providence of God, written on perishable parchment with pen and ink, liable to be lost or destroyed by fire, by natural decay and corruption, or by the enemies, whether civilized or pagan, that wasted and ravaged Christendom by the sword and gave its churches and monasteries and libraries to the flames.

Who, I ask, but the men and women, consecrated to God by their vows and devoted to a life of prayer and study in monasteries and convents, remote from worldly strife and ambition—who but they saved the written Word of God from total extinction and with loving and reverent care reproduced its sacred pages, to be known and read by all and to be handed down to our own generation, which grudges to acknowledge the debt it owes to their pious and unremitting labors?

IX

Bible Reading in the Dark Ages

B UT PERHAPS SOME OBJECTOR may say: "Yes, they copied the Scripture, these monks and priests, but that was all; they did not know anything really about it, did not understand it; their work was merely mechanical." I shall show that the contrary was the fact; they had a profound knowledge and understanding of the Bible, and it was their constant companion.

In the first place, the bishops and abbots required all their priests to know the Scriptures. We find constantly in the old constitutions and canons of different dioceses that the clergy were bound to know the psalms, the epistles, and Gospels, besides, of course, the missal and other Church service books (take for example, the constitutions of Belfric or of Soissons). These rules were effective; they had to be observed, for we find councils like that of Toledo, in 835, issuing decrees that bishops were bound to inquire throughout their dioceses whether the clergy were sufficiently instructed in the Scripture. In some cases they were obliged to know by heart not only the whole psalter, but (as under the rule of Pachomius) the New Testament as well.

When the clergy were continually meditating on various portions of the Scriptures, writing about them in homilies and commentaries, and ever reciting them in their services, they could not help but know them well. Some of the saints of those days, like Anselm and Hubert, actually knew them off by heart and could answer every question, however difficult, about the meaning of them. Not only saints, but multitudes of ordinary priests and bishops constantly had the Scriptures on their lips. Wulstan, bishop of Worcester, for example, had a custom, which would be decidedly trying to most clergy in our days, of repeating the whole psalter along with his attendant priests when journeying; we are told that "lying, standing, walking, sitting, he had always a psalm on his lips, always Christ in his heart." Again, we know of abbots (like him of Cologne) who "caused the whole of the Old and the New Testaments to be read through every year." Besides, the Scriptures were read daily during meals in monasteries.

If further proof were required that the clergy were intimately familiar, not only with the words, but with the meaning and teaching of Holy Scripture, we have only to dip into the sermons, happily preserved, which these men preached to their flocks, and we shall find them simply full to overflowing with quotations from every part of the Bible, far fuller, indeed, than the sermons of Protestant clergy in the twentieth century. I shall give only one example, and we have no reason to think that it is at all exceptional.

It is the sermon of a monk called Bardo in Germany, who was about to be appointed archbishop of Mentz. He preached first, however, before a great multitude at Christmas about the year 1000, the Emperor being present. His text was Psalm 17:3. I have not seen the whole of his sermon, but only about eight printed pages of it. I have counted the references and quotations from the Old and New Testaments, and I find there are exactly seventy-three. The audience enjoyed the sermon, understood the references, and the monk was made archbishop.

I hope I have shown now how really preposterous is the idea that the monks did not know the Bible. What man in his senses can have patience to listen to the silly legend that Martin Luther first discovered by accident the Scriptures—a book which, as a friar, he was bound to have known and studied and learned and recited for years? The simple fact, as is now proved by irrefutable evidence, is that the clergy of those "dark ages" had a knowledge of and familiarity with the written Word of God which modern ministers cannot equal; what is no less important, together with their knowledge they had a deep veneration and love for it, guarding it jealously from corruption and error, believing what they taught, humbly accepting its divine authorship and authority—an attitude in striking contrast to present-day critics, who treat the Bible like a common book, pick holes in it, impugn its genuineness and its accuracy, and in general attempt to eliminate the supernatural element from it altogether.

But, again, I think I hear the voice of the objector, who will not believe all this if he can possibly help it—"Yes, well, perhaps the clergy did know the Bible, but *nobody else did*; it was a closed and sealed volume to the poor lay people, because, of course, it was all in Latin."

Now, leaving aside the question of *Latin* for a moment (for I shall come back to that immediately), it is utterly false to say or suppose that the lay folks were ignorant of the Scriptures. They were thoroughly well-acquainted with them so far as they were required to be in their state of life. It is true, of course—and how could it be otherwise?—that ecclesiastics, being the reading men and writing men, in short, the only well-educated persons of those days, naturally have left behind them more evidence than most lay people could do of their familiarity with the Sacred Word, but it is yet the fact that the literature of those ages, outside clerical documents altogether, which has come down to us, is steeped and permeated through and through with Scripture. Conversations, for example, correspondence, law deeds, household books, legal documents, historical narratives—all are full of it, full not only of the ideas, but often of the very words of Scripture.

How many lawyers and doctors and professors and ordinary lay folks nowadays, I wonder, would be found quoting from the Bible in their writings? The reason, of course, was that books were scarce in those days and expensive, and the Bible was the most common and popular and accessible; it was the most familiar to kings and princes, to soldiers and lawyers, to businessmen and tradesmen, laborers and artisans. They all knew it and understood it, enjoyed the numberless quotations and references to it in sermons and addresses, and could often repeat portions of it from memory. "The writings of the dark ages"—says Dr. Maitland in chapter seven of his most valuable and entertaining book, *The Dark Ages*—"the writings of the dark ages are, if I may use the expression, made of the Scriptures. I do not merely mean that the writers constantly quoted the Scriptures and appealed to them as authorities on all occasions as other writers have done since their day, but I mean that they thought and spoke and wrote the thoughts and words and phrases of the Bible, and that they did this constantly and habitually as the natural mode of expressing themselves. They did it, too, not exclusively in theological or ecclesiastical matters, but in histories, biographies, familiar letters, legal instruments, and documents of every description. I do not know that I can fully express my meaning, but perhaps I may render it more clear if I repeat that I do not so much refer to direct quotations of Scripture as to the fact that their ideas seem to have fallen so naturally into the words of Scripture that they were constantly referring to them in a way of passing allusion which is now very puzzling to those who are unacquainted with the phraseology of the Vulgate."

We can thus see from the testimony of such a student of that period as Dr. Maitland how the language and ideas of the Bible had passed into the current language of the people. Sometimes persons carried copies of the Gospels about with them, just as Catholics today carry about them a Gospel of John, out of veneration.

But how, it may be asked, could the people who were unable to read (and they were admittedly a large number) become acquainted with the Bible? The answer is simple. They were taught by monk and priest, both in church and school, through sermon and instruction. They were taught by sacred plays or dramas, which represented visibly to them the principal facts of sacred history, like the Passion play of today at Oberammergau.

They were taught through paintings and statuary and frescoes in the churches, which portrayed before their eyes the doctrines of the faith and the truths of Scripture, and hence it is that in Catholic countries the walls of churches and monasteries and convents and even cemeteries are covered with pictures representing scriptural scenes.

"Painting is the book of the ignorant." Stained glass windows may be mentioned in the same category—and so may popular hymns, and poetry, and simple devotional books for the poor, all of which, along with the ceremonies and functions of the Church, served to imprint on people's memories and understandings the great events in God's dealings with his creatures since the beginning of the world. We must remember, too, that, for those who could not afford to purchase a Bible or a copy of the Gospels, the sacred volume was often chained to a stone in some public place about the church for everyone to study, and wealthy persons in their wills were known to leave money enough to provide for such a thing.

The simple truth is that the Catholic Church adopted every means at her disposal in these old days to bring a knowledge of God's Word to those who could not read, as well as to those who could. Bibles were not printed because there was no printing press; but whose fault was that? Is the Church to blame for not inventing printing sooner? But why did God not invent printing himself if he wished the Bible to be in everybody's hand? Nero had no motor car, nor had Julius Caesar a maxim gun, nor William Wallace a flying machine—were these men consequently ignorant and behind the times and worthy of contempt? There were no railway trains in Luther's day, nor did John Knox invent chloroform or Oliver Cromwell electricity—are these men in consequence to be considered as illiterate, stupid, barbarous, sunk in mental degradation?

The Catholic Church, then, had to do the best she could in the circumstances, and I submit she did all that any organization on earth could possibly have done for the spread of Scripture knowledge among her children. Vast numbers could not read; I admit it, but the Church was not to blame for that. Latin was the universal tongue, and you had to be rather scholarly to read it. But I protest against the outrageous notion that a man cannot know the Bible unless he can read it. Can he not see it represented before his eyes? Can he not hear it read? Do you not know and understand one of Shakespeare's plays much better by seeing it acted on the stage than by reading it out of a book? Do the visitors to Oberammergau, witnessing the Passion play, not come to understand and realize the story of the Passion and death of our Lord more vividly by *seeing* it enacted before their eyes than if they read the cold print of a New Testament? You hear a board school child rattling off the ten plagues of Egypt and the names of all the Kings of Israel and Judah, and various chapters of the Bible, but does that child necessarily know what he is reciting? Does he understand and appreciate and realize? He may or he may not; there is no necessary connection between the two things.

There is such a thing as literal idolatry, worshiping the letter and neglecting the spirit, a superstitious, groveling subserviency to the mere text of the Bible. A boy might know whole passages of the Bible by heart and only use them for his own moral ruin. I am contending for the genuine, real, practical working knowledge of the Bible among the generality of Catholics in the Middle Ages, and, whether they could read or not, I do not hesitate to assert that, with few exceptions, they had a personal and intelligent knowledge and a vivid realization of the most necessary facts in the Sacred Scripture and in the life of our divine Lord to an extent which is simply not to be found among the millions of our nominal Christians in these islands today. Whatever ignorance there was—this at least all impartial scholars must concede—the Church was in no way to blame for it.

Where, I ask, is the proof of the Church's hatred of the Bible, of any attempt to hide it, to destroy it, to dishonor and belittle it? I cannot do better than give you here two or three sentences from the work of the learned and honest Protestant student, some of whose words I have quoted before: "I must add that I have not found anything about the arts and engines of hostility, the blind hatred of half-barbarian kings, the fanatical fury of their subjects, or the reckless antipathy of the popes (in regard to the Bible). I do not recollect any instance in which it is recorded that the Scriptures, or any part of them, were treated with indignity or with less than profound respect. I know of no case in which they were intentionally defaced or destroyed (except as I have just stated for their rich covers), though I have met with, and hope to produce several instances, in some of which they were the only, and in others almost the only, books which were preserved through the revolutions of the monasteries to which they belonged, and all the ravage of fire, pillage, carelessness, or whatever else had swept away all the others. I know of nothing which should lead me to suppose that any human craft or power was exercised to prevent the reading, the multiplication, the diffusion of the Word of God."

We fittingly may conclude this part of our papers with the words of the *Quarterly Review*, October, 1879: "The notion that people in the Middle Ages did not read their Bibles is probably exploded except among the more ignorant of controversialists. The notion is not simply a mistake; it is one of the most ludicrous and grotesque blunders."

X

Where Are All the Medieval Bibles?

BUT LET US RETURN FOR A MOMENT to the popular objection (hinted at above): "Still the Bible was in Latin; you cannot deny that. The Church kept it in Latin so as the people should not read it. She was afraid of putting it into the common language of the people." There is some truth in these statements, but there is more untruth. That the Scriptures were for the most part in Latin is true; that it was because of the Church's dread of her people getting to know the Bible and so abandoning their Catholic faith is, of course, false.

1. Admitting for the moment that the Bible was in Latin during the Middle Ages, what follows? That nobody but priests could read it? Nonsense. There were just two classes of people then: those who could read and those who could not read. Those who did read could read Latin and, therefore, were perfectly content with the Scriptures in Latin. Those who could not read Latin could not read at all. I ask, therefore, what earthly need was there of a translation of the Bible from Latin into the language of the common multitude? What good would it have done?

At this point we may expect to hear our friend indignantly giving vent to some such objection as this: "The people, then, were horribly illiterate; they could not write their own names; they could not read; they were half barbarian and savage; they were really fearfully ignorant, you know, and degraded. Just compare them for one moment with our present-day school board children in the matter of reading and writing and general intelligence." Softly now, I answer; one thing at a time. We are not discussing that at present and do not mean to discuss it, because it is beside the question.

The Church was not to blame for the people's ignorance of letters; but let that pass, or even grant, if you like for the sake of argument, that the Church was blameworthy; the point I am insisting on is only this—granted a man cannot read, what on earth is the use of putting a Bible in his hand in any language under heaven, whether Greek or Hebrew, or Latin, or English, or Arabic? That man, if he is taught the Bible at all, must be taught it in other ways and by other means, as we have seen he was in the "Dark Ages." So that we arrive at this point, that either the Latin Bible was read or no Bible at all.

The learned Protestant author, Dr. Cutts, in his book *Turning Points of English Church History*, refers to this fact when he says: "Another common error is that the clergy were unwilling that the laity should read the Bible for themselves and carefully kept it in an unknown tongue that the people might not be able to read it. The truth is that most people who could read at all could read Latin and would certainly prefer to read the authorized Vulgate to any vernacular version" (preferred the Latin Bible to an English one.)

Dr. Peter Bayne also deals with this point when he remarks in *The Literary World* (October 1894), quoted by "M.C.L." in her booklet, "Latin was then the language of all men of culture and, to an extent probably far beyond what we at present realize, the common language of Europe; in those days tens of thousands of lads, many of them poor, studied at the universities and learned to talk Latin."

I may add that I came across the statement lately in the life of Peter Martyr, who flourished in the thirteenth century, that he gave some retreat or addresses to nuns in that age in Latin and was understood by them. The whole mistake in peoples' minds arises, of course, from the supposition they make that Latin was then a dead language, whereas it was really a living one in every sense of the term, being read and spoken and written universally in Europe and consequently being understood by everyone who could read at all.

What motive or purpose, then, could the Church have had in translating it into another tongue? In any case, this much none can help admitting—that at least the Church turned the Scriptures from Hebrew and Greek (which were the original languages) into Latin, which was the living language of the world, for the benefit of her children. She might still have kept the Bible a dark, unknown, mysterious document by leaving it in Hebrew and Greek. She did the very opposite. Does this seem as if she was anxious to keep her people in ignorance?

2. However, we are not done with objections yet. "How is it," ask our Protestant friends, "that if, as you say, the Sacred Scriptures were multiplied and reproduced and copied over and over again hundreds and thousands of times, even in Latin, how is it that we have so few of these copies now? Where have they gone? Surely we should expect to have many of them preserved." The question, I am afraid, betrays an ignorance (not altogether inexcusable) of the condition of society and civilization and of international relations in these distant centuries. There were many causes at work which perfectly account for the disappearance of the majority of the old copies of the Bible.

To begin with, there was frequent, if not continual, war going on, during which books and manuscripts were ruthlessly destroyed. We need only mention such instances as the invasions of the Danes and Normans, and of the Saracens and Northern Barbarians into Italy, burning monasteries and churches, sacking and laying waste to ecclesiastical buildings. During these oft-repeated incursions and the horrible pillage that generally accompanied warfare, many most valuable libraries and thousands of manuscripts and copies of the Scriptures of rare, indeed of priceless, worth must have perished.

Then there is the common occurrence of fire which accounts for the loss of much valuable literature—by which copies of Scripture were burned, either by accident or by design, either singly or in the general conflagration that consumed the whole monastery or library as well.

Another very common cause of loss was negligence, through which, both in the Middle Ages and since, many invaluable books and papers have gone to destruction. Sometimes a book was borrowed from the conventual library and never returned. This became so great an evil that proprietors of books adopted the plan of inscribing an excommunication or a curse against those who should keep or steal what had been merely lent—much in the style of the anathemas pronounced in the decrees of the Church's councils.

For example, we find one case like this: "This book belongs to St. Mary of Robert's Bridge; whosoever shall steal it or sell it, or alienate it from this house, or mutilate it, let him be anathema maranatha, Amen." The librarian was not often as careful as he should have been over his treasures, so his books and manuscripts were sometimes allowed to go a-missing, or to be taken away, or to perish through damp, or corruption, or rats or mice, or water, or by being stolen, or even by being sold by those who had no right to sell and to those who had no right to buy. Lastly, we know that great quantities of most important parchments and manuscripts have been used by bookbinders for such ignoble purposes as to form backs and bands and flyleaves and covers of other books.

But over and above these simple and natural causes, there was another which we must not forget and which was perhaps more far-reaching and powerful than the rest—I mean the deliberate destruction of the books and manuscripts so as to get the gold and silver and precious stones in which they were set and bound. I have spoken before of the costliness of the cases and ornaments that surrounded the copies of the Scriptures. Sometimes twenty pounds of pure gold were used in their binding, not to speak of the jewels that adorned their covers.

That rapacious and unscrupulous men, whether Catholic or Protestant, should in their lust for money seize upon these treasures, which were in the keeping of harmless and defenseless monks and priests, we can well understand; that they did so is unfortunately only too true. Thousands of monasteries and libraries were rifled, an incalculable amount of ancient and precious books and parchments burned or otherwise destroyed, their gold and silver settings turned into hard cash. For the Word of God they cared nothing; what they wanted was money. If this were true, as it is to a limited extent, of Catholic days, what shall we say of the robberies and plunders committed by sectaries in England, in their first fury, at the Reformation? We can scarcely conceive the extent to which the Reformers went in their rage and hatred against everything that had the least semblance of Rome about it, especially if it seemed likely to afford them some "filthy lucre." The Protestant historian Collier tells how Henry VIII, determined to "purge his library" of all popish and superstitious books, consequently gave orders for the destruction of such things as "missals, legends, and suchlike"; but notice the next point of command—"to deliver the garniture of the books, being either silver or gold, to his officers." That was the real motive: avarice, cupidity, greed of gold. The books thus plundered and stripped of their precious stones were largely Bibles and copies of the Gospels. Fuller says: "The Holy Scriptures themselves, much as the gospelers pretended to regard them, underwent the fate of the rest. If a book had a cross on it, it was condemned for popery, and those with lines and figures were interpreted the black art and destroyed for conjuring." "Whole libraries," exclaims another, "were destroyed or made waste paper of, or consumed for the vilest uses . . . broken windows were patched with remnants of the most valuable manuscripts on vellum, and the bakers consumed vast quantities in heating their ovens."

Collier, who is quoted above (he was an Anglican bishop), writes: "One among the misfortunes consequent upon the suppression of monasteries was an ignorant destruction of a great many books. The books, instead of being removed to royal libraries, to those of cathedrals or the universities, were frequently thrown into grantees as things of small consideration. These men oftentimes proved a very ill protection for learning and for antiquity; their avarice was oftentimes so mean and their ignorance so undistinguishing that, when the covers were somewhat rich and would yield a little, they pulled them off and threw away the books or turned them to wastepaper; thus many noble libraries were destroyed, to a great public scandal and an irreparable loss to learning." That Henry VIII caused the monasteries and convents to be dissolved, and their books and treasures plundered and pillaged wholesale, in order to replenish his coffers that were sorely depleted, is matter of history, though the ostensible reason was, of course, zeal for the true religion and the purifying of the morals of people and priests.

How far a sixteenth-century Nero like Henry VIII was fitted to undertake such a work is a matter of opinion. But certain it is that, in the diabolical fury which the authorities of that day waged against all Catholic institutions and monuments, loads of priceless copies of the Sacred Scriptures perished as utterly as though they had been destroyed by the pagan persecutors of the first four centuries after Christ. Listen (if you are not tired of hearing of such atrocities) to the account given by Dom Bede Camm, O.S.B., in his charming *Life of Cardinal Allen*, of the outrageous vandalism and hideous barbarities perpetrated at Oxford in those fearful days.

After telling how the chapel of All Souls was wrecked, its images and altars defaced and desecrated, the organs burnt in the quadrangle, and even the sacred pyx in which the body of the Lord had lain so long cut down and broken into pieces, he goes on: "Terrible, too, to all who loved learning was the wanton destruction of priceless manuscripts. Cartloads of books were carried off to the fire or sold to merchants to wrap their wares in. Anything which these miserable men did not understand was condemned as savoring of superstition.

All manuscripts that were guilty of the superstition of displaying red letters on their fronts or tiles were doomed. Ribald young men carried great spoils of books on biers up and down the city, singing as at a mock funeral, and their priceless burdens were finally burned in the common marketplace. The story of it all as told by contemporaries is all but incredible. The university library was stripped so bare that even the very shelves were sold for firewood, and the quadrangles of New College were for days littered with torn manuscripts."

I do not think I need say more on the point. It must be tolerably clear now where we should look for an answer to the question "Where are all the old copies of the Bible that Catholics say the monks so lovingly and laboriously made in the Middle Ages?" The answer must be plainly found in the insensate greed and fanatical destructiveness on the part of the sixteenth-century revolutionaries. Which side showed the more veneration and regard for God's written Word may be safely left to the judgment of all reflecting minds.

XI

Vernacular Scriptures before Wycliff

I HAVE SAID THAT PEOPLE WHO COULD READ at all in the Middle Ages could read Latin, hence there was little need for the Church to issue the Scriptures in any other language. But as a matter of fact she did in many countries put the Scriptures in the hands of her children in their own tongue.

1. We know from history that there were popular translations of the Bible and Gospels in Spanish, Italian, Danish, French, Norwegian, Polish, Bohemian, and Hungarian for the Catholics of those lands before the days of printing, but we shall confine ourselves to England, so as to refute once more the common fallacy that John Wycliff was the first to place an English translation of the Scriptures in the hands of the English people in 1382.

To anyone that has investigated the real facts of the case, this fondly-cherished notion must seem truly ridiculous; it is not only absolutely false, but stupidly so, inasmuch as it admits of such easy disproof; one wonders that nowadays any lecturer or writer should have the temerity to advance it.

Observe that I am speaking of the days before the printing press was invented; I am speaking of England and concerning a Church which did not, and does not, admit the necessity of Bible-reading for salvation and concerning an age when the production of the Scriptures was a most costly business and far beyond the means of nearly everybody. Yet we may safely assert, and we can prove, that there were actually in existence among the people many copies of the Scriptures in the English tongue of that day. To begin far back, we have a copy of the work of Caedmon, a monk of Whitby, at the end of the seventh century, consisting of great portions of the Bible in the common tongue.

In the next century we have the well-known translations of Venerable Bede, a monk of Jarrow, who died while busy with the Gospel of John. In the same (eighth) century we have the copies of Eadhelm, Bishop of Sherborne; of Guthlac, a hermit near Peterborough; and of Egbert, Bishop of Holy Island; these were all in Saxon, the language understood and spoken by the Christians of that time. Coming down a little later, we have the free translations of King Alfred the Great, who was working at the psalms when he died, and of Aelfric, Archbishop of Canterbury, as well as popular renderings of Holy Scripture like the Book of Durham and the Rushworth Gloss and others that have survived the wreck of ages.

After the Norman conquest in 1066, Anglo-Norman or Middle English became the language of England, and consequently the next translations of the Bible we meet with are in that tongue. There are several specimens still known, such as the paraphrase of Orm (about 1150) and the *Salus Animae* (1250), the translations of William Shoreham and Richard Rolle, hermit of Hampole (died 1349). I say advisedly "specimens," for those that have come down to us are merely indications of a much greater number that once existed but afterwards perished.

We have proof of this in the words of Thomas More, Lord Chancellor of England under Henry VIII, who says: "The whole Bible long before Wycliff's day was by virtuous and well-learned men translated into the English tongue, and by good and godly people with devotion and soberness well and reverently read" (*Dialogues* III). Again, "The clergy keep no Bibles from the laity but such translations as be either not yet approved for good, or such as be already reproved for naught [*i.e.*, bad, naughty] as Wycliff's was. For, as for old ones that were before Wycliff's days, they remain lawful and be in some folks' hand. I myself have seen, and can show you, Bibles, fair and old, which have been known and seen by the bishop of the diocese, and left in laymen's hands and women's too, such as he knew for good and Catholic folk, that used them with soberness and devotion."

2. But you will say, that is the witness of a Roman Catholic. Well, I shall advance Protestant testimony also.

The translators of the Authorized Version, in their preface, referring to previous translations of the Scriptures into the language of the people, make the following important statements. After speaking of the Greek and Latin versions, they proceed: "The godly-learned were not content to have the Scriptures in the language which themselves understood, Greek and Latin . . . but also for the behoof and edifying of the unlearned which hungered and thirsted after righteousness, and had souls to be saved as well as they, they provided translations into the Vulgar for their countrymen, insomuch that most nations under heaven did shortly after their conversion hear Christ speaking unto them in their mother tongue, not by the voice of their minister only but also by the written word translated."

As all these nations were certainly converted by the Roman Catholic Church, for there was then no other to send missionaries to convert anybody, this is really a valuable admission. The translators of 1611, then, after enumerating many converted nations that had the vernacular Scriptures, come to the case of England and include it among the others. "Much about that time" (1360), they say, "even in our King Richard the Second's days, John Trevisa translated them into English, and many English Bibles in written hand are yet to be seen that divers translated, as it is very probable, in that age. . . . So that, to have the Scriptures in the mother tongue is not a quaint conceit lately taken up, either by the Lord Cromwell in England [or others] . . . but hath been thought upon, and put in practice of old, even from the first times of the conversion of any nation." This testimony, from the preface (too little known) of their own Authorized Bible, ought surely to carry some weight with well disposed Protestants.

Moreover, the "Reformed" Archbishop of Canterbury, Cranmer, says, in his preface to the Bible of 1540: "The Holy Bible was translated and read in the Saxon tongue, which at that time was our mother tongue, whereof there remaineth yet divers copies found in old abbeys, of such antique manner of writing and speaking that few men now be able to read and understand them. When this language waxed old and out of common use, because folks should not lack the fruit of reading, it was again translated into the newer language, whereof yet also many copies remain and be daily found."

Again, Foxe, a man that Protestants trust, says: "If histories be well examined, we shall find, both before the Conquest and after, as well before John Wycliff was born as since, the whole body of Scripture by sundry men translated into our country tongue." "But as of the earlier period, so of this, there are none but fragmentary remains, the 'many copies' which remained when Cranmer wrote in 1540 having doubtless disappeared in the vast and ruthless destruction of libraries which took place within a few years after that date." These last words are from the pen of Rev. J. H. Blunt, a Protestant author, in his *History of the English Bible*; and another Anglican dignitary, Dean Hook, tells us that "long before Wycliff's time there had been translators of Holy Writ."

One more authority on the Protestant side, and I am done: It is Mr. Karl Pearson (*Academy*, August 1885), who says, "The Catholic Church has quite enough to answer for, but in the fifteenth century it certainly did not hold back the Bible from the folk, and it gave them in the vernacular a long series of devotional works which for language and religious sentiment have never been surpassed. Indeed, we are inclined to think it made a mistake in allowing the masses such ready access to the Bible. It ought to have recognized the Bible once for all as a work absolutely unintelligible without a long course of historical study and, so far as it was supposed to be inspired, very dangerous in the hands of the ignorant."

We do not know what Mr. Pearson's religious standpoint may have been, but he goes too far in blaming the Church for throwing the Bible open to the people in the fifteenth century or indeed in any previous age. No evil results whatsoever followed the reading of that precious volume in any century preceding the sixteenth, because the people had the Catholic Church to lead them and guide them and teach them the meaning of it. It was only when the principle of "private judgment" was proclaimed that the book became "dangerous" and "unintelligible," as it is still to the multitudes who will not receive the true interpretation of it at the hands of the Catholic Church and who are about as competent to understand and explain it by themselves as they are to explain or prophesy the movements of the heavenly bodies.

3. There is no need, it seems to me, to waste further time and space in accumulating proofs that the Bible was known, read, and distributed by the Catholic Church in the common language of the people in all countries from the seventh down to the fourteenth century. I have paid more attention to the case of England because of the popularity of the myth about Wycliff having been the first to translate it and to enable the poor blinded papists, for the first time in their experience, to behold the figure of the Christ of the Gospels in 1382.

Such a grotesque notion can only be due either to ignorance or concealment of the now well-known facts of history. One would fain hope that, in this age of enlightenment and study, no one valuing his scholarship will so far imperil it as to attempt to revive the silly fable. But supposing it were as true as it is false that John Wycliff was the first to publish the Bible in English, how in the name of reason can it be true at the same time that Luther, more than 100 years afterwards, discovered it? Really, people must decide which story they are going to tell, for the one is the direct contradictory of the other. Wycliff or Luther, let it be; but Wycliff and Luther together—that is impossible.

4. It may seem somewhat irrelevant to our present subject, which is simply "where we got the Bible," to wander off to foreign lands and see how matters stood there at the date at which we have now arrived, but I should not like to pass from this part of the inquiry without setting down a few facts which are generally unknown to our separated brethren, as to the existence of plenty of Bibles in those very countries which they think were, and of course still are, plunged in the depths of superstition, illiteracy, and degradation. They flatter themselves with the idea that it was the

knowledge of the Scriptures which produced the blessed Reformation the world over and will tell you that it was all because the Holy Book was sealed and locked and hidden away from the benighted papists in Continental countries that the glorious light of the Reformation never broke, and has not yet broken, upon them.

There are, however, unfortunately for them, facts at hand, facts unquestioned, which explode this pious notion. The facts are these:

As was shown long ago in the *Dublin Review* (October 1837), "It was almost solely in those countries which have remained constant to the Catholic faith that popular versions of the Bible had been published, while it was precisely in those kingdoms, England, Scotland, Sweden, Denmark, and Norway, where Protestantism acquired an early and has maintained a permanent ascendancy, that no printed Bible existed when they embraced Protestantism. Holland alone and a few cities in Germany were in possession of the Bible when they adopted the Reformed Creed." Is it really the case then, you ask with open eyes, that these Latin countries allowed the Bible to be read and translated and printed before Luther? Listen and judge for yourself what rubbish is crammed into people's heads.

Luther's first Bible (or what pretended to be the Bible, for he had amputated some of its members) came out in 1520. Now, will you believe it, there were exactly 104 editions of the Bible in Latin before that date; there were nine before the birth of Luther in the German language, and there were twenty-seven in German before ever his own saw the light of day. Many of these were to be seen at the Caxton Exhibition in London, 1877, and seeing is believing.

In Italy there were more than forty editions of the Bible before the first Protestant version appeared, beginning at Venice in 1471, and twenty-five of these were in the Italian language before 1500, with the express permission of Rome. In France there were eighteen editions before 1547, the first appearing in 1478. Spain began to publish editions in the same year and issued Bibles with the full approval of the Spanish Inquisition (of course one can hardly expect Protestants to believe this). In Hungary by the year 1456, in Bohemia by the year 1478, in Flanders before 1500, and in other lands groaning under the yoke of Rome, we know that editions of the Sacred Scriptures had been given to the people. "In all," (to quote from "M.C.L's" useful pamphlet on the subject) "626 editions of the Bible, in which 198 were in the language of the laity, had issued from the press, with the sanction and at the instance of the Church, in the countries where she reigned supreme, before the first Protestant version of the Scriptures was sent forth into the world."

England was perhaps worse off than any country at the time of the Reformation in the matter of vernacular versions of the Bible. Many Catholic kingdoms abroad had far surpassed her in making known the sacred Word. Yet these lands remained Catholic; England turned Protestant; what, then, becomes of the pathetic delusion of "Evangelical" Christians that an acquaintance with the open Bible in our own tongue must necessarily prove fatal to Catholicism? The simple truth of course is just this, that if knowledge of the Scriptures should of itself make people Protestants, then the Italian and French and Spanish and Hungarian and Belgian and Portuguese nations should all have embraced Protestantism, which up to the moment of writing they have declined to do. I am afraid there is something wrong with the theory, for it is in woeful contradiction to plain facts, which may be learned by all who care to take the trouble to read and study for themselves.

5. Before passing on to another part of the subject, I should like you to pause for a moment with the brief historical review fresh in your memory, and I would simply ask this: How can anyone living in the light of modern education and history cling any longer to the fantastic idea that Rome hates the Bible, that she has done her worst to destroy it, that she conceals it from her people lest it should enlighten their blindness, and that the Holy Book, after lying for many long dark ages in the dungeons and lumber rooms of popery, was at last exhumed and dragged into the light of day by the great and glorious discoverer, Martin Luther?

Do you not see that Rome could have easily destroyed it if she had been so disposed during all those centuries that elapsed between its formation into one volume in 397 and the sixteenth century? It was absolutely, exclusively in her power to do with it as she pleased, for Rome reigned supreme. What more simple than to order her priests and monks and inquisitors to search out every copy and reduce it to ashes? But did she do this?

We have seen that she preserved the Bible and multiplied it. She saved it from utter destruction at the hands of infidels and barbarians and pagan tribes who burned everything Christian they could come across; she saved it and guarded it from total extinction by her care and loving watchfulness—she and she alone. There was no one else to do it; she only was sent by God to defend his blessed Word. It might have perished, and would have perished, were it not that she employed her clergy to reproduce it and adorn it and multiply it and to furnish churches and monasteries with copies of it, which all might read and learn and commit to memory and meditate upon.

Nay, she not only multiplied it in its original languages (Greek and Hebrew), which would have been intelligible and useful only to the learned few, but she put it into the hands of all her people who could read, by translating it into Latin, the universal tongue; even for those less scholarly she rendered it into the common languages spoken in different countries. Truly she took a curious way of showing her hatred of God's Holy Word and of destroying it.

Many senseless charges are laid at the door of the Catholic Church, but surely the accusation that, during the centuries preceding the sixteenth, she was the enemy of the Bible and of Bible reading must, to anyone who does not willfully shut his eyes to facts, appear of all accusations the most ludicrous, and, to tell the truth, it is ridiculed and laughed out of court by all serious and impartial students of the question.

With far more justice, it humbly seems to me, may the charge of degrading and profaning the Sacred Scriptures be brought against those highly-financed Bible societies which, with a recklessness that passes comprehension, scatter among savages and pagans, utterly uninstructed, tons of Testaments, only to be used for making ball cartridges or wadding, for wrapping up snuff, bacon, tobacco, fruit, and other goods, for papering the walls of houses, for converting into tapestry or pretty kites for children, and for other and fouler uses which it makes one ashamed to think of. True, the versions thus degraded are false and incomplete, which may mitigate the horror in the eyes of Catholics, but those who thus expose them to dishonor believe them to be the real words of life. On their heads, then, falls the guilt of "giving that which is holy to the dogs."

XII

Why Wycliff Was Condemned

HERE WE ARE LIKELY TO BE MET with an objection by those who have not a very profound or accurate knowledge of the history of this question. They will say, "Why, if the Catholic Church approved of the Bible being read in the tongue of the people, why did she condemn Wycliff, one of her own priests, for translating it into English and forbid her people to read his version of the sacred Scriptures?" I answer, because John Wycliff's version of the Bible was not a correct version and because he was using it as a means of corrupting the people's faith and of teaching them false doctrine, and it seems to me at least that that was a perfectly good reason for condemning it.

1. Please observe that, while the Church approves of the people reading the Scriptures in their own language, she also claims the right to see that they really have a true version of the Scriptures to read and not a mutilated or false or imperfect or heretical version. She claims that she alone has the right to make translations from the original languages (Hebrew or Greek) in which the Bible was written, the right to superintend and supervise the work of translating, the right of appointing certain priests or scholars to undertake the work, the right of approving or condemning versions and translations which are submitted to her for her judgment. She declares she will not tolerate that her children should be exposed to the danger of reading copies of Scripture which have changed or falsified something of the original apostolic writing, which have

added something or left out something, which have notes and explanations and prefaces and prologues that convey false doctrine or false morals. Her people must have the correct Bible or no Bible at all.

Rome claims that the Bible is her book, that she has preserved it and perpetuated it, that she alone knows what it means, that nobody else has any right to it whatsoever or any authority to declare what the true meaning of it is. She therefore has declared that the work of translating it from the original languages, of explaining it, and of printing it and publishing it, belongs strictly to her alone and that, if she cannot nowadays prevent those outside her fold from tampering with it and misusing it, at least she will take care that none of her own children abuse it or take liberties with it, and hence she forbids any private person to attempt to translate it into the common language without authority from ecclesiastical superiors and also forbids the faithful to read any editions but such as are approved by the bishops.

All this the Catholic Church does out of reverence for God's Holy Word. She desires that the pure, uncorrupted gospel should be put in her people's hands as it came from the pen of the apostles and evangelists. She dreads lest the faithful should draw down upon themselves a curse by believing for gospel the additions and changes introduced by foolish and sinful men to support some pet theories of their own, just as a mother would fear lest her children should, along with water or milk, drink down some poison that was mixed up with it.

There are, let it be clearly understood, versions and versions of Holy Scriptures: some that are correct and guaranteed by the Church, others that simply bristle with mistakes and falsities. The former are permitted to Catholics to read and study; the latter, it need hardly be said, are utterly forbidden. To the latter class belonged the version of John Wycliff, first put into people's hands in 1382. A very slight knowledge of the man himself and of his opinions and of his career might persuade any reasonable person that a version made by him was the very last that would be allowed to Catholics.

2. What are the simple facts about the man? He was born in 1320, became a priest and theologian and lecturer at Oxford, and at first caused notoriety by taking part with the state against the claims of the pope in regard to tribute money and benefices. But in the course of a few years he went further and began to oppose the Church not only in matters of policy or government (a course which might conceivably at times be pardonable), but in the things of faith. Being accused of preaching novel and uncommon doctrines, he was, at the instance of Pope Gregory XI, summoned before his archbishop in 1378 and inhibited from teaching any further on the matters in dispute.

No more proceedings were taken against him (though he did not desist from his anti-papal teaching) till 1381, when again he was making himself notorious. He attacked the friars and religious orders with great bitterness, impugned transubstantiation and seemed to advocate the theory that was afterwards peculiarly Luther's, ridiculed indulgences and flooded the country with pamphlets and tracts reeking with heresy. He was, in short, a kind of Lollard. "The Lollards" (says the *National Cyclopaedia*) "were a religious sect which rose in Germany at the beginning of the fourteenth century and differed in many points of doctrine from the Church of Rome, more especially as regards the Mass, extreme unction, and atonement for sin."

That, of course, is a very bald and crude statement of their tenets. The extent of their "differences from the Church of Rome" will appear in a clearer light if we consider the "Lollards' Petition to Parliament," 1395. It contained among other novelties the famous "twelve conclusions" against the temporal possessions of the Church, the celibacy of the clergy, and all vows of chastity, against exorcisms, blessings of inanimate objects, transubstantiation and prayers for the dead, pilgrimages, compulsory auricular confession, veneration of images, and the holding of secular offices by priests. Many also objected to the taking of oaths, denied the necessity of baptism for salvation, held marriage to be a mere civil contract, and spoke of sacramentals as "jugglery." (See *Chambers Cyclopaedia* and *The Catholic Cyclopaedia*, under "Lollards.")

You may sympathize with these amiable persons if you like, but you would hardly expect the Catholic Church of that century (or of any century) to sympathize with them and still less to suffer them to issue her Scriptures expurgated according to their ideas. But thus did John Wycliff. "He held views" (says the devout Anglican, Dore, in his most interesting work *Old Bibles*), "which, if carried into practice, would have been totally subversive of morality and good order, but he never separated himself from the [Catholic] Church of England."

Another Anglican says the Lollards were political martyrs rather than religious, that their actions tended to a revolution in the state as well as in the Church, and that both civilians and ecclesiastics regarded their principles as subversive of all order in things temporal as well as things spiritual (Dr. Hook, *Lives of Archbishops of Canterbury*).

Can we be surprised, then, at reading that in 1382, in consequence of the heresies that he was now spreading, John Wycliff was again put on trial by the ecclesiastical courts and that twenty-two propositions taken from his works were condemned? Thereupon he retired to Lutterworth, of which he had been rector for many years.

He was gently dealt with, and his declining years were not harassed by any of the persecution and torture which it pleases some to depict him as suffering, and he died, after a stroke of paralysis while hearing Mass, on December 31, 1384. In later years, two separate councils, one at London, the other at Constance, selected forty-five propositions from the teaching of Wycliff and condemned them, declaring some to be notoriously heretical, others erroneous, others scandalous and blasphemous, others seditious and rash, and the rest offensive to pious ears.

3. I ask any unprejudiced person, Was this the kind of man to undertake the translation of the Bible into the common language of the people? Was he likely to be trusted by the Church at that time to produce a version thoroughly Catholic and free from all error or corruption—a man notoriously eccentric, guilty of heretical and suspicious teaching, attacking the Church in its authorities

from the pope down to the friars, and associated with sectaries abroad who were at once revolutionaries and heretics? The question answers itself. You may cry out that Wycliff was right and Rome was wrong in doctrine, that he was a glorious Reformer and "morning star of the Reformation," and that he taught the pure word of the Lord as against the abominable traditions of the Scarlet Woman of Babylon.

But I humbly submit that that is not the point. The point is this: You ask, Why did the Catholic Church condemn Wycliff's version and at the same time allow other versions of the Bible in English? and I am showing you why. I am telling you that Wycliff was heretical in the eyes of Rome, that he produced a heretical version for the purpose of attacking the Catholic Church of that day and of spreading his heresies, and that to blame the Church for forbidding him to do so, and for condemning his version, is about as sensible as to blame an author for interdicting someone else from publishing a copy of his work that was full of errors and absurdities and that contained opinions and sentiments which he detested.

The Catholic Church certainly could never allow a version of Holy Scripture (which is her own book) like that of Wycliff to go forth unchallenged, as if it were correct and authoritative and bore her sanction and approval. As well might we expect the British sovereign to sanction some hideous caricature from a comic paper as a true and faithful picture of his coronation.

4. We do not shrink from giving John Wycliff and Nicholas of Hereford an equal share of praise for their laborious work of translating the whole of the Bible into the English tongue, if the work was really theirs (which some scholars such as Gasquet, however, have doubted). What we assert is that it was a bad translation and hence useless, and worse than useless, for Catholics. It was condemned and forbidden to be used by a decree, of Archbishop Arundel at Oxford in 1408, which also prohibited the translation of any part of the Bible into English by any unauthorized person and the reading of any version before it was formally approved.

This was a natural and wise and necessary decree. It did not forbid the reading of any of the *old approved versions* of Scripture in English which existed in great numbers before Wycliff, as we have seen already. Nor did it forbid new versions to be made or read, if under proper supervision and approval by ecclesiastical superiors. It banned only false and unauthorized translations like Wycliff's; Protestant writers, such as Dr. Hook, have often declared their belief that it was not from hostility to a translated Bible as such that the Church condemned Wycliff and that she never would have issued her decree if his sole purpose had been the edification and sanctification of the readers. It was only when the design of the Lollards was discovered, and Wycliff's subtle plot unmasked of disseminating their pestilential errors through his translation, that the Church's condemnation fell upon him.

A greater authority even than Dr. Hook, I mean the veteran historian Dr. James Gairdner—an English Churchman who spent more than sixty of his fourscore years in research among the state papers of England dealing with the period about the Reformation and who was recognized as easily the most profound and comprehensive student of those times—Dr. Gairdner, I say, expressed some very strong conclusions to which his historical inquiries had driven him in regard to the Wycliffite revolt and its results and about Rome and the Bible. (See his book *Lollardy and the Reformation*, reviewed in *The Month*, December 1908.)

"The truth is," he says, "the Church of Rome was not at all opposed to the making of translations of Scripture or to placing them in the hands of the laity under what were deemed proper precautions. It was only judged necessary to see that no unauthorized or corrupt translations got abroad; and even in this matter it would seem the authorities were not roused to special vigilance till they took alarm at the diffusion of Wycliffite translations in the generation after his death."

Again, "To the possession by worthy lay men of licensed translations the Church was never opposed; but to place such a weapon as an English Bible in the hands of men who had no regard for authority, and who would use it without being instructed how to use it properly, was dangerous not only to the souls of those who read, but to the peace and order of the Church."

From a deep, calm scholar like Dr. Gairdner words like these are more valuable than whole volumes of partisan and unenlightened assertions from anti-Catholic controversialists, and (as Fr. Herbert Thurston suggests) we cannot but feel grateful to this honored old scholar in the evening of his days for thus vigorously and boldly identifying himself with an unpopular cause. Simply honesty of purpose and love of truth compelled him, out of his vast and prolonged studies, to expose the revolutionary character of the Wycliffite and Lollard rebellions against Rome, as well as to sympathize with the glorious martyrs such as More and Fisher, and to defend the Catholic authorities such as Archbishop Wareham and Bishops Bonner and Tunstall, and to vindicate the good reputation and piety of the monasteries so cruelly suppressed by Henry VIII. But we are anticipating. I was speaking of the Church's condemnation of Wycliff's undesired and undesirable version.

5. This was the first time in England that the Church ever felt herself obliged to lay some restriction on Bible reading in the vulgar tongue, and that fact in itself is surely sufficient to prove that there must have been some very special reason for her acting so differently from what she had been accustomed to do before. Her action at this time was precisely similar to the action of the Church in France nearly two hundred years previously.

Then (in the twelfth and thirteenth centuries) some heretics called Waldenses and Albigenses revolted against all authority and overran the country, spreading their wild and blasphemous doctrines. They taught, among other enormities, that there were two Gods (creator of the good and creator of the evil), that there was no Real Presence of our Lord in the Blessed Eucharist, that there was no forgiveness for sins after baptism, and that there was no resurrection of the body. They declared oaths unlawful, condemned marriage, and called the begetting of children a crime. All these impieties they professed to base on Holy Scripture.

Consequently, to save her people from being ensnared and led away, the Church, in council assembled at Toulouse in 1229, passed an enactment forbidding to laymen the possession of the sacred books, especially in the vernacular, though anyone might possess a breviary or a psalter or office of our Blessed Lady for devotion. Will anyone blame the Church for taking these measures to suppress the poisonous heresy and prevent its spreading and to save the Sacred Scriptures from being made the mere tool and war cry of a certain sect? In like manner we may not blame the Church at Oxford under Archbishop Arundel for her famous constitution against Wycliffite and other false versions of the Bible, but rather admire and applaud her wisdom and vigilance and zeal for the purity of the gospel of Jesus Christ.

In the same way we may examine and investigate the action of the Church in various countries and in various centuries as to her legislation in regard to Bible reading among the people, and wherever we find some apparently severe or unaccountable prohibition of it, we shall on inquiry find that it was necessitated by the foolish or sinful conduct on the part either of some of her own people or of bitter and aggressive enemies who literally forced her to forbid what in ordinary circumstances she would not only have allowed but have approved and encouraged.

It is true that the approving or condemning of Bible reading in particular centuries or countries is a matter of policy and of discipline on the part of the local Catholic authorities. It depends largely upon the prudence and wisdom and zeal of the bishops set over them and does not necessarily involve any action on the part of the pope as supreme head of the Church. Hence one cannot declare infallibly offhand that there has never been a case of unwise or indiscreet legislation in regard to the matter at the hands of individual bishops.

I do not know of any case myself and never read of any instance where bishops have been proved in the course of time to have made mistakes in issuing decrees about the matter. Supposing some mistake had been made, that would not affect the general principle on which the ecclesiastical authorities always are supposed to act; in the light of Rome's principle and her clear and definite attitude towards the Bible as her own book, we may safely challenge anyone to convict her either of inconsistency or hatred towards God's written Word.

Once grasp her doctrinal position in regard to the Bible and the rule of faith, and you will have no difficulty in accounting for her uncompromising hostility to versions like Wycliff's and for her action in condemning the Bible societies which spread abroad a mutilated, corrupt, and incomplete copy of the Holy Scriptures (generally accompanied by tracts) with the design of undermining the faith of Catholics.

XIII

Tyndale's Condemnation Vindicated

S
O MUCH THEN FOR JOHN WYCLIFF and his unhappy version. The next man of any consequence we are confronted with is another favorite of the Reformers, another "martyr" for the Bible, and that is William Tyndale. His treatment is also flung in our teeth by critics, as fresh evidence of Rome's implacable hatred of the open Bible. Did she not persecute and burn poor Tyndale and consign his copy of the Scriptures in English to the flames? So here again we must show how wise and consistent was the action of the Catholic Church in England in regard to Tyndale and his translations and clear her absolutely from the slightest shadow or suspicion of hostility to God's written Word.

1. What we are about to speak of now, be it remembered, is the printed Bible, for in 1450 the art of printing was discovered by a man rejoicing in the melodious name of Johann Gutenberg (a German), and in 1456 the first book ever printed issued from the press at Mainz, and it was—what? It was the Bible, and it is known as the Mazarin Bible, after Cardinal Mazarin. This demonstrates anew what hatred Catholics had in those days toward the Bible, and their fear and dread lest it should be known even to exist! The best way to keep it secret, of course, was to print it.

Besides, how could the Bible be printed in 1456? Did not Martin Luther discover it for the first time in 1507? However, joking apart, the fact remains that we have now in our historical review arrived at the point where we bid farewell to copies of the Bible written by the hand and have to consider only those that were turned out by the printing press from 1456 onwards. On Protestant principles it must seem a pity that the Lord waited so many centuries before he invented printing machines to spread Bibles about among the people, and it seems also very hard on all preceding generations that slipped away without this lamp to their feet and light unto their path.

2. William Tyndale was born in 1494, eleven years after Martin Luther was born and one hundred and ten years after John Wycliff died. He studied at Oxford, became a priest, and was seized with the ambition of getting the Bible printed in England. There were three great objections to this step being approved.

In the first place, Tyndale was not the man to do it; he was utterly unfitted for such a great work. He says himself he was "evil favored in this world and without grace in the sight of men, speechless and rude, dull, and slow-witted." He had no special qualifications for the task of translation. He was but a mediocre scholar and could not boast of anything above the average intellect. Indeed, non-Catholic authors have admitted that the cause of Scripture reading in the vernacular was distinctly prejudiced by having been taken in hand by incapable men like Tyndale.

In the second place, he was acting entirely on his own account and without authorization from ecclesiastical superiors, either in England or in Rome; he was simply a private, obscure priest and was acting without commission and without sanction from higher quarters. Indeed, I go further and say that he was acting in disobedience to the decision of higher authorities.

At the very beginning of the sixteenth century (I am now quoting the Anglican Doré) "the authorities of the English Church took into consideration the desirability of introducing a vernacular Bible into England, and the great majority of the Council were of opinion that, considering the religious troubles on the Continent and the unsettled state of things at home, at this juncture the translation of the Bible into the vulgar tongue, and its circulation among the people, would rather tend to confusion and distraction than to edification."

You may lament if you like (as Doré does) this decision as an error of judgment and affirm that the postponement of an English version in print authorized by the bishops was a most unfortunate event, as leading to false and corrupt versions being issued by irresponsible individuals. But right or wrong in their judgment, this was the conscientious conclusion at which the council under Archbishop Wareham arrived: No printed English Bible meanwhile was to be allowed, and, after all is said and done, they were probably better judges than we are as to what was best for the Church of that time in England. The Lutheran revolution was in full swing abroad (1520), and the Lutheran heresy was spreading everywhere, carrying with it rebellion and immorality, and the English bishops might well have cause to fear lest the infection should poison the faithful under their own jurisdiction.

In the third place, there was no demand for a printed English Bible to any great extent—certainly not to the extent of making it at all an urgent or pressing duty on the part of the authorities to issue one. Doré (so often quoted already) ridicules the idea that at that time England was a "Bible-thirsty land." He declares that "there was no anxiety whatever for an English version excepting among a small minority of the people," and "the universal desire for a Bible in England we read so much of in most works on the subject existed only in the imagination of the writers."

Dr. Brewer, another Protestant, also scoffs at the idea. "To imagine," he says, "that ploughmen and shepherds in the country read the New Testament in English by stealth, or that smiths and carpenters in towns pored over its pages in the corner of their master's workshops, is to mistake the character and acquirements of the age." There has, in short, been a great deal of wild and groundless talk about the intense desire of the people of that century to devour the Scriptures.

We can prove it by these simple facts, that the people had to be compelled by law to buy Bibles, for acts were passed again and again threatening the King's displeasure and a fine of forty shillings per month if the book was not purchased; we have documentary evidence that inhabitants of certain parts of the country, such as

Cornwall and Devonshire, unanimously objected to the new translation and that even among the clergy Reformers such as Bishop
Hugh Latimer almost entirely ignored the English copy and always
took their texts from the Latin Vulgate; printers had large stocks
of printed Bibles left unsold on their hands and could not get rid
of them at any price, except under legal coercion; the same edition
of the Bible was often reissued with fresh titles and preliminary
matter, and new title-pages were composed for old unsold Bibles,
without any regard to truth, simply to get them sold.

I do not see how we can resist the conviction that there was
really no extensive demand for English Bibles among the mass of
Christians at that time in England, whether clergy or laity, and that
the design of spreading them wholesale among the masses was borrowed from the Continent, which was then in a perfect ferment of
religious and civil revolution. Hence you can understand at once
how Tyndale's proposal was viewed with suspicion and disfavor by
the bishops and himself refused any assistance or encouragement
from Tunstall, bishop of London, and other prelates.

When we further bear in mind (as the *Athenaeum* pertinently
remarked, August 24, 1889) that this irresponsible private chaplain
had become already known as a man of dangerous views, who was
exceedingly insulting in his manner, unscrupulous, and of a most
violent temper, that in postprandial discussions he repeatedly
abused and insulted Church dignitaries who were present, that with
him the pope was Antichrist and the Whore of Babylon, while the
monks and friars were "caterpillars, horse-leeches, drone-bees, and
draff," we shall not be vastly astonished that these dignitaries did
not evince much enthusiasm in pushing on Tyndale's scheme.

3. Unable therefore to proceed with the work in his own land
because of ecclesiastical prohibition, Tyndale goes abroad and after
much wandering about settles at Worms, where in 1525 the Bible
was printed and thence smuggled in considerable quantities into
England. At once, as was to be expected, it was denounced by the
bishop of London, and I do not deny (nor can I see any reason to
deplore) the fact that copies of it were burned ceremonially at St.
Paul's Cross. But why? Because it was a false and erroneous and

anti-Catholic version of the Holy Scriptures. It was full of Lutheran heresies. Tyndale had fallen under the influence of the German Reformer, who by this time had revolted from Rome. About 1522 Tyndale had been suspected and tried for heresy; he had declared: "I defy the pope and all his laws." Now he actually embodied in his English version Luther's notes and explanations of texts, which were as full of venom and hatred against Rome as an egg is full of meat.

"It has long been a notorious fact," says Mr. Allnatt (in his *Bible and the Reformation*), "that all the early Protestant versions of the Bible literally swarmed with gross and flagrant corruptions—corruptions consisting in the willful and deliberate mistranslation of various passages of the sacred text and all directly aimed against those doctrines and practices of the Catholic Church which the 'Reformers' were most anxious to uproot. They did give the people an 'open Bible,' but what a Bible!"

Canon Dixon, the cultured Anglican historian, referring to the fact that copies of Tyndale's Bible were burnt, makes these striking remarks: "If the clergy had acted thus simply because they would have the people kept ignorant of the word of God, they would have been without excuse. But it was not so. Every one of the little volumes, containing portions of the sacred text that was issued by Tyndale, contained also a prologue and notes written with such hot fury of vituperation against the prelates and clergy, the monks and friars, the rites and ceremonies of the Church, as was hardly likely to commend it to the favor of those who were attacked."

Tunstall, bishop of London, declared he could count more than 2,000 errors in Tyndale's Bible "made in Germany," while the learned Sir Thomas More, Lord Chancellor of England, found it necessary to write a treatise against it and asserted that to "find errors in Tyndale's book were like studying to find water in the sea." In short there is not an unprejudiced inquirer now but admits that the Church could not possibly tolerate Tyndale's Bible as though it were a true or correct version of the Holy Scriptures.

She had no alternative but to prescribe and forbid it, otherwise she would have been sinfully neglectful of her guardianship over the Word of God and of idly standing by while her children were being poisoned. But who will be so obtuse or so malicious as to twist this action of hers into a determined hatred of the Scriptures *as Scriptures* and to represent her as hostile and opposed to all reading of the Bible whatsoever, even of a true and correct version? Surely to hate the Bible is one thing, and to prohibit a false version of the Bible is quite another.

Has the Catholic Church not as a matter of fact put a correct copy of the Bible into the hands of her children in their own language in the Douay version? As for the burning of Tyndale's version, there is nothing to be wondered at in it; it was probably the only or at least the most striking and effective way of stemming its sale and instilling a horror of it into the hearts of the people. It was the custom of the age (as Doré remarks) to burn the works of opponents, as Luther a few years before burnt the books of canon law, and the bull of Pope Leo and in 1522 John Calvin burnt all the copies he could collect of Servetus' Bible at Geneva, because these contained some notes he did not think were orthodox. Indeed Calvin went a step further than that—he burned Servetus himself. Surely it must be plain enough to everyone that, in the case before us, what the ecclesiastical authorities meant to destroy was not the Word of God, but the errors of Luther and Tyndale which were corrupting it.

4. But the most interesting point about the whole affair is that time has abundantly justified the action of the Catholic Church and proved that she did the proper thing in attempting to stamp out Tyndale's Bible. The reading of this pernicious book produced most disastrous effects upon the morals of the people, who became rebellious, profane, irreligious, and disaffected to the civil as well as to the spiritual authorities.

Hence we find that for ten years Tyndale's version was denounced and opposed even more by the court and secular officials than by the bishops, and that at least two royal proclamations were issued for every clerical one, against all who read or concealed the obnoxious volume. In fact in the year 1531 King Henry VIII, with the advice of his council and prelates, published an edict that "the translation of the Scripture corrupted by William Tyndale should be utterly expelled, rejected, and put away out of the hands of the people, and not be suffered to go abroad among his subjects." What a commentary upon the good and godly doctrines inculcated by Mr. William Tyndale!

Some years later (the King's veto not having secured the desired effect), after several other editions of the English Bible had been issued and the condition of the Scripture-reading masses was becoming worse and worse in consequence, the same royal Defender of the Faith caused another act to be passed (1543) entitled "for the advancement of true religion and for the abolishment of the contrary." By force of this it was decreed that, seeing what abuses had followed the indiscriminate reading of certain versions of Holy Scripture, what "tumults and schisms," "divers naughty and erroneous opinions," and "pestiferous and noisome teachings and instructions" had sprung up, including "writings against the holy and Blessed Sacrament of the Altar, and for the maintenance of the damnable opinions of the sect of Anabaptists"—all to the "great unquietness of the realm and great displeasure of his Majesty" as a result of all this—it was enacted that "all manner of books of the Old and New Testament in English, being of the crafty, false, and untrue translation of Tyndale," along with any writings containing doctrine contrary to that of the King, "shall be clearly and utterly abolished, extinguished, and forbidden to be kept or used in this realm."

The act then goes on to explain what versions of the Bible might be used, and by whom, and forbids the general reading of it by women, artificers, journeymen, and certain other classes; it lays down sundry other restrictions in regard to it, which are to be observed, under pains and penalties, ranging from fines of 40 shillings up to imprisonment for life.

I shall not dwell on the reflections that arise in one's mind on reading such legal enactments coming from such a man as Henry VIII, but, to complete our remarks about Tyndale's version and to pursue to the end the King's dealing with it, I may add that the very year before he went to his account (1546) he struck one more blow, which no doubt he intended to be and hoped would be fatal, at this hated volume. He deliberately commanded all copies of it (along with Coverdale's) to be delivered up and burned. Verily the "whirligig of time brings in his revenges." After this, one finds it somewhat amusing to be told that only priests and popes burn and hate the Word of God. Henceforth Protestant readers of these lines would do well to remember that the great Reformer and founder of the Church of England, Henry VIII, set a high example in the matter. However, that is by the way. I was saying that the time justified the action of the Church, which first proscribed and did its utmost to repress Tyndale's version, and I have shown how the secular power felt itself driven in self-protection to do the same.

But another, and perhaps to Protestants a more telling, proof of the statement is found in the fact that their subsequent versions of Scripture deliberately omitted Tyndale's most characteristic features, such as his notes, prefaces, and prologues. They appeared and then they disappeared. They had their day, and they ceased to be. They were considered unfit to find a place in what purported to be a pure copy of the work of the apostles and evangelists. Posterity, then, has justified Sir Thomas More and has condemned Tyndale. What is this but to vindicate the Church in her action toward the corrupt volume? Wisdom is indeed "justified of her children."

XIV

A Deluge of Erroneous Versions

FOLLOWING TYNDALE'S EXAMPLE, others continued the work of issuing English-printed Bibles, and so in the reign of Henry VIII we have to face quite a deluge of them. One by one they came forth, authorized and unauthorized, printed and published by irresponsible individuals, full of errors, with no proper supervision and having no other effect (as we shall presently see) than that of drawing down contempt and disgrace upon the Sacred Scriptures.

1. The English Church was now separated from Rome, and the English bishops were mere puppets and slaves at the beck and call of the royal tyrant, Henry. They exercised no real independent jurisdiction over either clergy or people; the governor and ruler in Church and state was the king, and consequently no ecclesiastic could undertake responsibility in regard to the publication or suppression of Bibles without the will of his imperial master. So long as Henry made no objection, any printer or publisher or literary hack, who thought he saw a chance of making a little money out of the venture, would take in hand the publishing of a new version of the Bible.

George Joye, for example, took this course in regard to Tyndale's Bible and in consequence (1535) brought down upon himself a volley of bitter and un-Christian reproaches from that worthy who (as I have said before) was a man of uncontrollable temper and scurrilous language when thwarted or resisted.

In reply to this tirade, George Joye published an "Apology," in which he showed that the printer had paid him only four-and-a-half pence for the correction of every sixteen leaves, while Tyndale had netted £10 for his work; and besides, he exposed in fine style the departure from the truth of which Tyndale had been guilty in boasting of his translation and exposition as if it were his own, whereas Joye shows it was really Luther's all the time, that Tyndale did not know enough Greek to do it and had only added "fantasies" and glosses and notes of his own imagination to the work of others. However, we have no time to dwell on the quarrels of these amiable Bible translators, else we should never reach the end of our historical review. Let us enumerate briefly the versions that saw the light in rapid succession during the reign of Henry VIII.

2. There was Myles Coverdale's in 1535. Coverdale was a priest who married abroad and kept a school. In after years King Edward VI granted him and his wife, Elizabeth, a dispensation to eat flesh and white meats in Lent and other fasting days. It is wonderful what power the kings of England had in those days!

In 1537 appeared Matthew's or Rogers' Bible (which was a mixture of Tyndale's and Coverdale's), and this has the distinction of being the first that Henry authorized to be used by the people at large. Matthew or Rogers (for he assumed different names for Bible-selling purposes) was, like Coverdale, a renegade priest and had married, and we are not surprised to find that some of his notes on the gospel were indecent, and others consisted of abuse of the Church, her clergy, and her doctrines.

Two years later (1539), Taverner produced another version of the Bible. He was a layman, but a preacher notwithstanding, who had saved his skin by recanting his opinions. The same year appeared a version that was to hold the field for popularity for the next twenty years, the Great Bible, sometimes called Cranmer's, from the preface written by that accommodating prelate. It was Cromwell (Thomas, not Oliver, of course) who engineered it and Coverdale who supervised its progress. The printing of it was begun in France, but when the work was half finished, the inquisitor general very properly stepped in and confiscated the presses and types.

If England was going to the dogs through anti-papal Bibles, he saw no reason why France should do the same. However, it was completed and published in London in 1539, and, like previous versions, contained fulsome flattery of Henry VIII, concerning whom our Lord is represented as saying, "I have found a man after my own heart, who shall fulfill all my will!"

This volume was by royal proclamation ordered to be put up in every church in England, and Bonner, bishop of London ("Bloody Bonner"), who is held up as the most determined enemy of Bible reading, set up at his own expense six beautiful copies of this book at various convenient places in St. Paul's Cathedral. Unfortunately, so much ill-feeling, disturbance, contention, and irreverence was the result of this unrestrained Scripture reading that he was compelled to threaten their removal.

The license to read and judge, each one for himself, of the sense and meaning of the Word of God produced, as we said before, most lamentable effects and led to the utter degradation of the sacred volume. Not that there was any eager desire or thirst for it or any great or general use made of it, for the printers often complained of the large stock left, unbought, on their hands, and begged that persons should be compelled to purchase them, and besought that no fresh editions might be published. We have seen that acts had to be made to force people to buy them, under threat of fine and imprisonment. But yet those who did read the Bible made it only a matter of altercation and contention and argument and brought it down to the depths of disrepute and contempt.

The extent to which this evil had spread may best be judged from the pathetic lament of Henry VIII himself in his last speech to Parliament: "I am extremely sorry to find how much the Word of God is abused, with how little reverence it is mentioned, how people squabble about the sense, how it is turned into wretched rhymes, sung and jangled in every alehouse and tavern, and all this in a false construction and counter-meaning to the inspired writers. I am sorry to perceive the readers of the Bible discover so little of it in their practice, for I am sure charity was never in a more languishing condition, virtue never at a lower ebb, nor God himself less honored or worse served in Christendom." There is no ambiguity about these words, and when we remember that the same sentiments are expressed in the writings and speeches of many of the Reformers themselves, who complain of the licentiousness of the masses since the abolition of popery, and remember how Henry VIII was constrained to seize and burn Tyndale's and Coverdale's and other versions of the Bible and to forbid the reading of any version at all to large classes of his subjects—in the face of all this, who will fail to see the sinful folly of the policy of the English schismatics of that day? Who will deny that the Catholic Church showed consummate wisdom, holy prudence, and the truest reverence for God's Word in withholding her version till a more convenient season?

3. But are we finished with the erroneous versions yet? Far from it. Henry VIII certainly authorized no more, for the simple reason that he went to Judgment in 1547. No new edition came out in Edward VI's reign (1547–1553), but in 1557 one was published that owed its origin to William Whittingham, a layman, who had married a sister of John Calvin's wife and who was made Dean of Durham. Whittingham's Bible, issued at Geneva, perpetuated the corruptions of Tyndale's with an epistle of Calvin added to the epistles of Paul and the other apostles.

During the reign of "Bloody Mary" (1553–1558), who, of course, ought to have hated the Scriptures like poison (being a bigoted papist and the wife of a Spaniard), there were, strange to say, no proclamations against Scripture reading, nor is there to be found any trace of opposition on the part either of the queen or of her bishops to the Bible being read or printed in the vulgar tongue; so says Mr. Blunt, the Anglican historian.

With the accession of the "Virgin Queen Bess," however, a new Bible saw the light in 1560 at Geneva. It was the work of the Nonconformists resident there and is known as the Genevan Bible, though Bible collectors know it more familiarly by the title "Breeches Bible," from its rendering of Genesis 3:7: "They sewed fig leaves together and made themselves breeches." It was certainly the most popular that had yet appeared among the sectaries, partly because of its undeniable scholarship and accuracy and partly because of its notes on the margin, which were fiercely Calvinistic. Take an example: Revelation 9:3. Here the note runs: "Locusts are false teachers, heretics, and worldly subtle prelates, with monks, friars, cardinals, patriarchs, archbishops, bishops, doctors, bachelors, masters, which forsake Christ to maintain false doctrine." Nobody worth speaking about is missed out here.

The Puritan soldiers used to carry about with them a little book made up of quotations from the notes of this Calvinistic version. It seems also to have suited the Scottish taste of the period, for it was the first edition printed in Scotland. So little, however, did the great mass of the people in this country care for any Bible in English at all that the Privy Council passed a law compelling every householder possessed of a certain sum to purchase a copy under a penalty of £10. The magistrates and town council of Edinburgh also did their best to force the sale of the volume, and searchers went from house to house throughout this unhappy land to see if it had been bought.

But, in spite of all the pressure, we find from the Privy Council records that many householders preferred to incur the pains and penalties to purchasing the Bible. An old dodge was adopted in regard to the Genevan version that had done service with previous copies—the dodge, namely, of issuing the very same book, with the same errors and identical notes, but under a new title page, so as to deceive the unwary into believing it was a fresh edition. This trick had to be played, of course, by the unfortunate and impecunious printers and booksellers, who had large stocks of Bibles unsold on their shelves, and the perpetration of this fraud helped the Genevan editions considerably.

The Elizabethan bishops soon found that this Bible, with its violent Calvinistic notes and teaching, was undermining the popularity of the Church of England, so Matthew Parker, archbishop of Canterbury, set himself the task of providing another version that would be less offensive to the High Church party and more favorable to Anglicanism. The result was the Bishops' Bible, which appeared in 1568 and took the chief place in the public services of the Church, though it never displaced the Genevan in the favor of the people.

We are close now to the moment at which the first Catholic version (and up till today the only one ever sanctioned in English) appeared. But there was still one more Protestant version which, as it is yet the principal recognized Bible of the Protestants of the British Empire, must not be omitted. I mean, of course, King James's version of 1611. It is the three-hundredth anniversary of this, commonly called the Authorized Version, that English-speaking Protestants are everywhere celebrating this year (1911).

4. Neither the royal pedant himself [James] nor anybody else seems to have been satisfied with any of the Bibles then floating about. Dr. Reynolds, the Puritan leader, "moved his Majesty there might be a new translation of the Bible, because those which were allowed in the reign of Henry VIII and Edward VI were corrupt and not answerable to the truths of the original." James, great scholar as he thought himself to be, professed "that he could never yet see a Bible well translated into English, but the worst of all his Majesty thought, the Geneva"—a judgment we cannot be surprised at, considering that that version openly allowed disobedience to a king and blamed Asa for only deposing his mother and not killing her (Chron. 15:16).

Moreover, he declared that "some of its notes were very partial, untrue, seditious, and savored too much of dangerous and traitorous conceits." Hence a large band of translators was appointed, and in 1611 there was finished and published what has proved to be the best Protestant version that ever appeared—one which has exercised an enormous influence not only on the minds of its readers, but also on English literature throughout the world. In 1881–1885 this version of King James was revised, but, while acceptable to students, the revision has gained no hold upon the people at large.

5. How long it will be before another Protestant version appears he would be a bold man who would venture to prophesy, but that others will spring up and add to the number of the wrecks that already strew the path we may confidently predict. I have given a goodly list of corrupt and erroneous versions, but please do not

imagine for a moment that my catalogue is anything like complete. I have merely mentioned those that were more commonly used and secured a certain amount of popularity and authorization from Protestant headquarters. But there are, I am safe in saying, hundreds of other editions that flooded this unhappy realm from the time of Tyndale, some from foreign countries, like Holland, Germany, and Switzerland, and some produced at home, but all of them swarming with blunders and perversions.

On glancing over a bookseller's catalogue the other day my eye happened to light on some of those that have attained notoriety for their absurd mistakes. There is, for example, the "He" Bible and the "She" Bible, so called from the hopeless mixing up of these pronouns in the book of Ruth; the "He" Bible has one set of errors and the "She" Bible another. There is the "Wicked" Bible from the word "not" being omitted from the Seventh Commandment. There is the "Vinegar" Bible, from printing "vinegar" instead of "vineyard," and so producing "The Parable of the Vinegar." This Bible was printed by a man called Baskett and is now vainly sought for by collectors on account of its numberless errors; indeed, it was wittily called the "Baskett-ful of Errors." There is the "Murderer's Bible," from the words of our Lord being thus printed: "But Jesus said unto her, let the children first be killed" (instead of "fed"). Then we have the "Whig" Bible and the "Unrighteous" Bible and the "Bug" Bible and the "Treacle" Bible and no end of other kinds of Bibles, all crammed full of mistakes and corruptions. The "Pearl" Bible, for instance, published by Field, the Parliamentary printer, has 6,000 errors in it. A famous book was written by a man named Ward in the seventeenth century, entitled *Errata of the Protestant Bible*, contains a formidable list of I should not like to say how many thousand errors in the various versions. No one has yet succeeded in refuting Ward's *Errata*. It stands as a gruesome commentary on the history of heretical treatment of the inspired text.

I came across a curious and rare book one day in Glasgow University Library. It was written in 1659 by a Protestant, William Kilburn, and entitled *Dangerous Errors in Several Late Printed Bibles to the Great Scandal and Corruption of Sound and True Religion*.

He enumerates the errors, omissions, and specimens of nonsense that he discovered in these editions, many of them imported from Holland, and mentions that a gentleman had unearthed 6,000 mistakes in one copy alone.

6. But time would fail to tell of all the corruptions and perversions of the original texts which are to be found in practically all the Protestant Bibles, down to the present time, and whose existence is proved by the fact that one after the other has been withdrawn and its place taken by a fresh version, which in its turn was found to be no better than the rest. Is this reverence for the Word of God?

Which of all these corrupt, partisan versions was "the rule of faith"? The Bible, and the Bible only, we are told—but which Bible? I ask. Or had Protestants a different rule of faith according to the century in which they lived, according to the copy of the Bible they chanced to possess? What a mockery of religion! What a degradation of God's Holy Word, that it should have been knocked about like a shuttlecock, and made to serve the interests now of this sect, now of that, and be loaded with notes that shrieked aloud party war cries and bitter accusations and filthy insinuations! Is this zeal for the pure and incorrupt gospel? Is this the grand and unspeakable blessing of the "open Bible"? It only remains now to show by contrast the calm, dignified, and reverent action taken by the Catholic Church toward her own book.

XV

The Catholic's Bible

WHAT WAS THE CATHOLIC CHURCH doing all this time? Well, she was in a state of persecution in England and could not do very much except suffer.

1. Many of her best sons went abroad to more favorable lands. The circumstances had assuredly been most unsuitable for bringing out a Catholic version of the Scriptures. She was rather content, indeed compelled, to sit still and from her majestic height look down and watch the rise and fall, the publication and withdrawal, the appearance and disappearance of dozens of different versions, heretical and corrupt, grotesque in their blunders and bitter in their sectarianism, that had been issued by the various bodies.

By the end of the sixteenth century no less than 270 new sects had been enumerated, and some that had been extinct for centuries, like Arianism, revived under the genial influence of Luther. Dr. Walton, bishop of Chester and author of the famous polyglot Bible that bears his name, laments this fact in his preface at the end of the seventeenth century.

"There is no fanatic or clown," says he, "from the lowest dregs of the people who does not give you his own dreams as the Word of God. For the bottomless pit seems to have been set open from whence a smoke has risen which has obscured the heavens and the stars, and locusts are come out with wings—a numerous race of sectaries and heretics, who have renewed all the old heresies and invented monstrous opinions of their own. These have filled our cities, villages, camps, houses—nay, our churches and pulpits, too, and lead the poor deluded people with them to the pit of perdition."

Doubtless the poor bishop, being a self-complacent Anglican, failed to perceive that he himself was as much of a deluded sectary and heretic as any of them. It was not till 1582 that a Catholic New Testament appeared, and that was not in England, but in France, at Rheims, whence a colony of persecuted Catholics had fled, including Cardinal Allen, Gregory Martin, and Robert Bristow, who were mainly responsible for this new translation. William Allen, formerly canon of York, later archbishop of Mechlin, and lastly cardinal, had founded a college at Douay in 1568 for the training of priests for the English mission. He was compelled to remove it to Rheims in 1578 owing to Huguenot riots, and there, as I said, in 1582 they issued the New Testament in English for Catholics.

It was a translation, of course, from the Latin Vulgate, which had been declared by the Council of Trent to be the authorized text of Scripture for the Church. Martin was the principal translator, while Bristow mainly contributed the notes, which are powerful and illuminative. The whole was intended to be of service both to priests and people, to give them a true and sound rendering of the original writings, to save them from the numberless false and incorrect versions in circulation, and to provide them with something wherewith to refute the heretics who then, as ever, approached with a text in their mouth.

2. Needless to say, the appearance of this New Testament, with its annotations, at once aroused the fiercest opposition. Queen Elizabeth ordered the searchers to seek out and confiscate every copy they could find. If a priest was found in possession of it, he was forthwith imprisoned. Torture by rack was applied to those who circulated it, and a scholar, Dr. Fulke, was appointed to refute it. All these measures, be it noted, kind reader, were taken by parties who advocated loudly the unlimited right of private judgment.

In 1593 the college returned to Douay, and there in 1609 the Old Testament was added, and the Catholic Bible in English was complete, and is called the Douay Bible. Complete we may well call it; it is the only really complete Bible in English, for it contains those seven books of the Old Testament which I pointed out before, were and are omitted by the Protestants in their editions. We can claim to have not only the pure, unadulterated Bible, but the whole of it, without addition or subtraction: a translation of the Vulgate, which is itself the work of Jerome in the fourth century, which, again, is the most authoritative and correct of all the early copies of Holy Scripture.

At a single leap we thus arrive at that great work, completed by the greatest scholar of his day, who had access to manuscripts and authorities that have now perished and who, living so near the days of the apostles and, as it were, close to the very fountainhead, was able to produce a copy of the inspired writings which, for correctness, can never be equaled.

We may feel justly proud of our Douay Bible. We need not declare it to be perfect in all respects, either in regard to its English style or its employment of words from foreign languages; we need not feel the less affection or admiration for it though we should suggest the possibility of revision and improvement in some particulars—it has, indeed, been reedited and revised ere now especially by Bishop Challoner. But when all is said and done, it is a noble version with a noble history: true, honest, scholarly, faithful to the original.

The Catholic Church has nothing to regret in her policy or her action toward English versions of the Scriptures. She has not issued one version one year and canceled it the next because of its corruptions and errors, its partisan notes, or its political doctrines. Nobly she has stood for reverence and caution in respect of translating God's Holy Word into the vulgar tongue. She was slow in acting, I admit, if by slowness we mean deliberation and prudence, for she saw with unerring vision the evils that were certain to result from haste. But when she did act, she acted decisively and once for all.

Who is there that has followed the sad story of the non-Catholic treatment of the Sacred Scriptures but will be forced by contrast to admire the wisdom, the calm dignity, the consistent and deliberate policy of the ecclesiastical authorities of the Catholic Church in England, which stands as a reproof to the violent, blundering, malicious methods of the sectaries and which, if it had been acquiesced in by others, would have saved the Word of God from infinite degradation and contempt?

3. Hatred against her version of the Bible when it first appeared was so deep that an oath sworn on it was not deemed to be valid. It was on the Rheims New Testament that Mary, Queen of Scots, laid her hand and swore her innocence the night before her execution. The Earl of Kent at once interposed with the remark that the book was a popish and false translation and in consequence the oath was of no value. "Does your Lordship suppose," was the quiet answer of the noble queen, "that my oath would be the better if I swore on your translation, which I do not believe?"

Thanks be to God, the Douay version has now so established its position, and hatred to it and to its authors has so diminished, that a Catholic may, even in these lands, swear upon it in conscience, and his word is believed as any other man's in a court of law. Found in thousands of pious Catholic homes at the present hour, we may comfort ourselves with the reflection that, in this kingdom, there has now for long existed the true version of the gospel of our Blessed Lord and the inspired words of his holy apostles and evangelists, as they have been handed down and preserved by the Catholic Church from the beginning, unchangeable and unchanged. We may feel the most absolute certainty that, as it is the true version, so, at a date not incalculably distant, it will prove to be the only one, for the others will have gone to join their predecessors, and been consigned to a happy oblivion, and only survive in the memory of him who glances at their musty covers and faded pages beneath the glass cases of library or museum.

XVI

Envoi

M Y TASK IS FINISHED, and you, dear reader, if you have followed it up, will utter, I am sure, a hearty *Deo gratias!* As sincerely and as clearly as possible, I have tried to show that it is to the Catholic Church under God that we owe the preservation and integrity of the Sacred Scriptures.

The Old Testament she took over from the Jewish Church; to it she added the New Testament, the work of her own apostles and bishops, and, comprising them in one great whole, declared that they had the Holy Ghost for their author and were neither to be increased nor diminished. Throughout the ages when there was no other Church she has preserved them from error, saved them from destruction, multiplied them in every language under heaven, and put them with the necessary prudence in her people's hands. Again and again heretics and apostates have tried to mutilate and corrupt them—indeed, have actually done so—but the Roman Church has ever preserved a version pure and entire.

She claims that she alone knows the meaning of their teaching and alone possesses the right to interpret them to men. She will tolerate no tampering with the sacred text, and in these days especially, when scientists and critics who have lost belief in the supernatural attack them and labor to overthrow their divine authority and authorship, Rome alone stands as their protector; to her alone lovers of the sacred volume, be they Catholic or Protestant, must look to save it and defend it. The papacy has appointed a standing

Biblical Commission to guard the integrity and authenticity of Holy Scripture. This is but natural; the Bible is the Church's offspring. But it is surely the keenest irony of history that, while Protestants themselves are striving with might and main to pull to pieces the ancient object of their veneration, the Catholic Church, ever reputed its deadliest enemy, alone is left of all Christian bodies to save it from destruction. This she will do, as she has ever done in the past; it is part of her office in this world; there is no other that has either the right or the power to do it. If the Bible loses its sovereign place in the hearts and minds of non-Catholics, as it is rapidly doing, it is the work of those who, whether in Germany, or Britain, or America, have loudly professed themselves its greatest champions.

The Catholic Church, on the other hand, in her long history has nothing to be ashamed of in her treatment of it, but deserves the praise and thanks of all Christians for so zealously and fearlessly protecting it from corruption and contempt. Indeed, I will say that a simple study of her attitude towards the inspired Scriptures, in comparison with that of all other bodies, will furnish one of the strongest arguments that she is the True Church of Christ.

Venerable and inspired as Catholics regard the Bible, great as is their devotion to it for spiritual reading and support of doctrine, we yet do not pretend to lean upon it alone, as the rule of faith and morals. Along with it we take that great Word that was never written, Tradition, and hold by both the one and the other interpreted by the living voice of the Catholic Church speaking through her supreme head, the infallible Vicar of Christ. Here we have a guide that has never failed, and never can, in teaching us our duty both to God and man.

Not on the quicksands of human and varying judgment, but on the rock of divine authority we place our feet. Amid the warring of opinions and the conflict of numberless editions and versions of Sacred Scripture and the confused and contradictory interpretations of texts, we find an unassailable refuge in the decision of Rome. In submitting to the judgment of that Church to which Christ gave divine authority to teach when he said, "Go ye and teach all nations," we find a sure consolation and an abiding peace.

Individual interpretation of the Bible—the most sublime but also the most difficult book ever penned—can never bring satisfaction, can never give infallible certainty, can never place a man in possession of that great objective body of truth which our Blessed Lord taught and which it is necessary to salvation that all should believe. It can not do so because it was never meant to do so. It produces not unity, but division; not peace, but strife. The experience of many centuries proves it.

Only listening to those to whom Jesus Christ said, "He that heareth you heareth me," only sinking his own fads and fancies and submitting with childlike confidence to those whom the Redeemer sent out to teach in his name and with his authority—only this, I say, will satisfy a man and give to his intellect repose and to his soul a "peace that surpasseth all understanding." Then no longer will he be tormented with contentious disputings about this passage of the Bible and that, no longer racked and rent and "tossed to and fro with every wind of doctrine," changing with the changing years. He will, on the contrary, experience a joy and comfort and certainty that nothing can shake in being able to say, "O my God, I believe whatever thy Holy Catholic Church believes and teaches, because thou hast revealed it who canst neither deceive nor be deceived."

God grant that many Bible-readers and Bible-lovers may obtain the grace to make this act of faith and pass from an unreasoning subservience to a book to reasonable obedience and submission to its maker and defender—the Catholic and Roman Church.

From the Kirk
to the Catholic Church

Foreword

E VERY SCOTSMAN OF OPEN MIND and good will, Catholic and non-Catholic alike, will welcome the re-publication of the pamphlet *From the Kirk to the Catholic Church*, produced by the Reverend Bishop Henry G. Graham fifty years ago, shortly after his ordination to the priesthood. It is a religious autobiography of great interest, written in a simple, direct, and confidential tone, by which the young Fr. Graham sought to lay open before his friends the reasons and the motives and the workings of divine Providence which had brought to him the happiness of homecoming to the Church. It established for his contemporaries the strength and the sincerity of his convictions, and it provided himself with a vehicle by which to express his gratitude to Almighty God for the grace of conversion.

The conversion of a son of the manse to the ancient Catholic faith was a rare event indeed in the first decade of the century, and Henry G. Graham was not only a son of the manse, but was himself a minister and the last of a long unbroken line of Grahams who had ministered in the Kirk throughout two centuries. This is therefore a kind of apology, but it is an apology not in the debased sense of that word as we use it commonly today, but in the sublime and positive sense in which the word is used by Plato and by Cardinal Newman.

It may well be hoped that this little work will help many to see in right perspective the issues involved in the Scottish Reformation.

The clear mind and deep learning of the bishop, even as a young priest, enabled him to set forth these issues with brilliant clarity, and his charity impelled him to give to others the opportunity of finding the happiness which God had given him.

All Catholics in Scotland are grateful to the Catholic Truth Society for providing us with this memorial to a great and much beloved priest and bishop.

James Black
Bishop of Paisley
February 23, 1960

From the Kirk to the Catholic Church

FOR NEARLY THREE HUNDRED AND FIFTY YEARS Scotland has been a dry and barren land, from the Catholic point of view. By the Act of 1560, the old religion was abolished and the Kirk formally set up. Confiscation and imprisonment followed the first offense of saying or hearing Mass; banishment overtook the second, and death the third. To all intents and purposes, Catholicism was simply wiped out of the country. A mere handful of Highlanders was all that remained to represent a Church which had once reigned supreme throughout the kingdom and had the spiritual allegiance of every living soul from John o' Groats to the Solway.

So things continued until quite recent days. Very few conversions took place; they could hardly be expected. Hatred of Rome was too intense, and ignorance of her history and doctrines too profound, to permit of them. Scarcely anybody thought even of inquiring into the Catholic faith. Conversion was a thing practically undreamt of, and, if the idea was entertained, the inquirer was bound to remember that the step involved persecution and perhaps banishment. We require to come to the nineteenth century, and even to the second half of it, before we find any notable revival of the faith or increase in the number of Catholics. Even this can hardly be said to be owing, to any appreciable extent, to conversions, but rather to the immigration of the Catholic Irish.

Of late years, however, there has been a movement in the valley of dry bones, as in the day of the Prophet Ezekiel (Ezek. 37:7), and a noise and a shaking, and the Lord God has caused the breath of life to breathe upon them, and the bones have come together, and the sinews and the flesh, and many of the slain have risen again and stood upon their feet. It is life from the dead. From a dead Protestantism has sprung a little army of living Catholics.

There has been a steady accession of converts to the faith, and of these "recruits of Rome" many have come in through sheer force of conviction, brought about by prayer and study and travel and personal investigation into the Catholic system wherever it could be seen at work. From the ranks of the nobility and gentry, from among university men and professors, from the legal and medical professions, and from all the working classes, converts have been entering the fold.

There has been no deluge or downpour of conversions—perhaps it is better so, meanwhile—yet the drops have been falling in tolerably quick succession, giving hopes of a pretty heavy shower at a date not too distant, let us hope, for the readers of these lines to be refreshed by it.

We may not be impatient. To become a Catholic, we should bear in mind, is always a great venture of faith; it is especially so among a people like the Scotch, so crassly ignorant of the Catholic Church and invincibly prejudiced against her. Hence it is only with much fear and trembling, with many a haunting dread and many a wistful look behind, that converts in Scotland have hitherto ploughed their way into the fold.

But the doubters and inquirers are now plucking up courage. They have seen others going into the kingdom of heaven before them, and, what is stranger still, stopping there; they know how happy these have been as Catholics; they have watched them for years and years, and even until death, persevering in the faith of Rome and enjoying a peace, a comfort, and a satisfaction they never found before. Seeing this, they are emboldened themselves to begin and try to do likewise.

Among these, there is a class I have not mentioned yet, and that is the clergy of the Presbyterian churches. They, too, have furnished some converts, but so far they have been very few. Theologically speaking, they are hard nuts to crack. Slow, hardheaded, cautious, unemotional, like the rest of their race; suckled and reared on Calvinism; inheriting a profound horror of Rome and all her ways; suspicious of the least tendency toward Catholicity and consequently devoid of the smallest disposition to inquire—it will at once be seen that ministers are not the kind of material out of which converts are readily to be made.

Being, besides, mostly married men with families, they have, according to the familiar saying, many weighty arguments against turning over to the Catholic Church. The father of the writer of these lines, for example, possessed ten such arguments. "I have married a wife, and therefore I cannot come" may still be urged as an excuse by others than the man in the parable.

Considering Presbyterianism, moreover, as the acme of respectability, the symbol of honesty and manliness, and a sure guarantee of worldly prosperity and independence, its reverend officials, with equal assurance, consider Catholicism to stand for filth and degradation, for lying and dishonesty, and look upon it as the sure forerunner of temporal decadence, intellectual stagnation, and spiritual bondage. It may be good enough for the Irish, but Scotsmen are entitled to something higher. So deeply ingrained in their minds is such a sentiment that a common argument wherewith to dissuade young persons from becoming Catholics is to reproach them with bringing disgrace upon an honorable family and dragging down their father with gray hairs in sorrow to the grave.

Parental claims and filial affection are herein set up in conflict with the voice of conscience, and the average son and daughter would require more than the average moral courage and strength of will to let conscience gain the victory. "You might at least have some respect for your people, if you have none for yourself," was the rebuke addressed to an accomplished Presbyterian lady, suspected of "Roman leanings" and detected coming out of a Catholic church in the month of September in the city of Edinburgh in the year of grace 1909.

Tenfold greater, naturally, would be the shame if the family were that of a minister. Ministers themselves, as I remarked before, are not very likely converts; there is probably no class of people less happily situated for acquiring Catholic sympathies or less amenable to conviction as to the Catholic claims. Conscious though many of them are of the defects and weaknesses of their own system, they yet instinctively, and at the very outset, put Catholicism out of the question as a sheer impossibility, as hateful to God and loathsome to men. Not that way is to be sought the solution of any of their difficulties.

Their roots are firmly struck in a form of Protestantism—the Presbyterian system—deeply antagonistic to any authority except the Bible and utterly opposed to submitting to the decision of any superior court other than one's own conscience. To tear himself up by the roots and transplant himself in other soil—a thing which every convert is, in a manner, forced to do—would be for the ministerial convert a work of rare and almost insuperable difficulty.

Human respect, intellectual pride, inherited prejudice, traditional associations, domestic and financial considerations together with an unconquerable and unreasoning dread of the supremacy of Rome—these and others that could be named are certainly motives which deter many from passing over to her embrace. When it is remembered, further, that there is no point of similarity or contact whatsoever between Catholicism and Presbyterianism, that the two systems are separated and opposed as the poles asunder, that in the public services and devotions of the Kirk there is absolutely nothing bearing the least resemblance to Catholic observance or ritual, and that, in consequence, the ministers are destitute of even that superficial inkling as to Catholic worship which Anglicans enjoy—I say when one remembers these points, one can scarcely be surprised that Catholicity has made so few conquests among them; the wonder rather is that she has reaped any at all.

Yet there have been some, and there will soon be more. As the present writer has had the happiness, by the grace of God, of becoming one of her recruits in these days, he is willing to recount in the simplest way possible the various steps that led him from the darkness of heresy to the light of the truth, in the hope that others may be encouraged to make a like inquiry, and, fearing nothing, to "follow the gleam" until it grows and brightens for them into the full blaze of divine truth and floods their souls with the heavenly light that streams from the Catholic faith. Then will they be able to say with the psalmist: *"In lumine tuo videbimus lumen"* ("In your light we see the light" [Ps. 36:9]).

Home

I had a poor chance of knowing anything about the Catholic Church, for my father was then pastor of a parish where papists were as rare as snakes in Ireland. In the summer and autumn, indeed, one met numbers of Irishmen who had come to Scotland for the harvesting operations, but we never thought or asked about their religion. At the school I attended there were, of course, no Catholic pupils, although in the train in which we traveled to and from the town we occasionally met a priest. My ignorance, therefore, of Catholicism could not have been more complete, and I passed from the school to the university in 1889, a common or orthodox Presbyterian—whatever that may import.

Both at day school and at Sunday school we certainly had been taught to know the Bible well, especially the historical parts, and had learned large portions of it off by heart, as well as many of the metrical psalms and paraphrases of Scripture which are appended to the Bibles intended for Scottish consumption. Prizes were given for "searching the Scriptures" and for answering biblical questions and puzzles, which involved a deal of concordance-hunting.

Needless to say, we each possessed a Bible of our own, and, true to the Scotch genius and tradition, we seemed to be more familiar with the Old than with the New Testament. Small illustrated books, giving the chief Bible stories in popular style for children, such as *Line upon Line* and *Little by Little*, were much in use. I well remember how our youthful imagination was delighted with pictures of Samson pulling down the house upon the heads of the Philistines and Aod thrusting his dagger into fat King Eglon, and Jael hammering a nail through the brain of Sisera while he lay asleep.

Sunday was a horribly dull day, for, taking Scotland generally, it was, to all intents and purposes, simply the Jewish sabbath. My father did not, indeed, belong to "the most straitest sect of our religion," those, I mean, who on the "sabbath" assumed long faces, kept their window-blinds down, and refused to cook a hot dinner. He was rather of the "Moderates" who had kicked against this excessive Puritanism and had introduced organs, or "kists o' whistles," into their services. Yet were we not allowed to read any but religious books on Sunday, or to whistle, or go beyond the grounds appertaining to the manse. I need scarcely add that we did all these forbidden things from time to time.

Twice a year a fast day was observed, when some "strange minister" came and preached to a half-empty church, to prepare the parishioners for the Lord's Supper on the Sunday following. There was no fasting, however, on these occasions, though there had been in former days.

Young folk communicating for the first time were admitted at this season; when about sixteen years old I joined with the rest, but I cannot say that any deep impression was made upon my soul. The chief meaning of the act seemed to be that we were "joining the church" for the first time—coming out as church members, publicly demonstrating our Christian faith, and, like the Jewish boys presenting themselves at the Temple, taking upon ourselves the responsibility of keeping the law of God.

Moreover, the whole teaching about the sacrament being a "sign and seal," and about "receiving Christ by faith," and about "feeding upon Christ crucified and all benefits of his death" was so vague and insubstantial that my mind was in a fog regarding it, and I suspect that the great majority of the communicants were, and are, equally befogged. In the popular estimation, it was and is nothing more than a memorial feast, recalling the Last Supper and our Lord's sufferings and death. Though some of the clergy would fain exalt its meaning and attribute to it some higher efficacy, the people generally regard their "going forward to the tables" simply as a demonstration of their church membership and as keeping in memory the death of Christ. If they reach any deeper or higher, they will be touching on a spiritual Communion, which is the farthest extent they can go.

Terrible warnings used to be uttered against "eating and drinking unworthily," and many would approach in fear and trembling lest they should be guilty of the unpardonable sin. But the "fencing of the tables" in my day was a weak and paltry thing in comparison to what it used to be, when the unworthy were denounced in terms that struck terror, if not compunction, to the hardest hearts. The conditions for partaking were made so strict that whole classes of people shrank back lest they should be profaning the Lord's table. Jansenists and Presbyterians could here meet on common ground.

On Sunday mornings and evenings we would have family prayers and on Sunday nights, in addition, hymns and sacred music, of which my father was very fond, being a musical enthusiast and indeed a composer of hymn tunes not at all contemptible. So far as one's private prayer is concerned, I have no distinct recollection what forms we used, beyond the Lord's Prayer with the long ending, "For Thine is the kingdom and the power and the glory for ever. Amen," and a childish rhyme to this effect:

> *This night when I lie down to sleep,*
> *I pray to the Lord my soul to keep;*
> *If I should die before I wake,*
> *Take me to heaven for Jesus' sake.*

Anything like the Catholic acts of faith or hope or charity or of sorrow for sin was, of course, utterly unknown.

As for the Church, we were trained in our histories to think that the Reformation was a glorious thing for the country, to revere its heroes such as John Knox and the "good Regent" Stewart, and to admire Elizabeth while abhorring "Bloody Mary." Being the descendant of a line of ministers in direct succession for more than two hundred years, I naturally looked upon the Established Kirk as the ideal of a church and grew to conceive a wholesome contempt for all dissenting bodies, of which, however, there were none in our parish.

So far as theology was concerned, our heads were, of course, crammed with Calvinism; for years after I went to college I simply accepted it, like any other youngster, without criticism or reflection. I grew up in the Reformed faith, and under Presbyterian government and worship, without asking whether it was right or wrong and knowing and caring nothing about Catholicism or Anglicanism. All the doctrines of the Reformers—including such superficialities as God's eternal decrees, election, foreordination, justification, and effectual calling—were instilled into our minds, but not in a controversial way. I must admit that we were never taught to hate Rome or Roman Catholics; indeed, such a subject was never mentioned at all. We learned nothing further about our differences with the Roman creed than might be picked up from some occasional answer in the *Shorter Catechism*, such as that which had to be explained in our preparation for our first Communion.

Calvinistic theology is a most thorny and controversial subject, even among those who profess to accept it, and I recollect, while a lad, puzzling my brain and hunting through musty tomes of Scottish divines to find some reconciliation between St. Paul's supposed doctrine of justification by faith and St. James's doctrine of justification by works. It goes without saying that I found no reconciliation, because there was nothing to reconcile.

I was very early destined for the ministry of the Kirk and encouraged to believe that the aim of my life should be to follow my father's footsteps and perpetuate the ministerial succession which had been in the family for so many generations. This is the only kind of apostolic succession, I may remark, which is possible in Protestant churches. To "wag your head in a pulpit" was considered the highest pinnacle of honor to which a Scotsman could attain.

I was the youngest of five sons, and, as none of the others had been good enough (or bad enough) to do this wagging, my father's hopes in this direction were fixed on me. I responded quite readily to the idea, not being aware of anything that would suit me better, and therefore, as before stated, at the age of fifteen I was bundled off to the university and safely lodged under the pious wing of a young divinity student.

College

A Scotch university is not a very religious place. Neither professors nor students need have any religion unless they like—there are no tests—and, as a matter of fact, a great many have none except that of nature. The only teachers who are bound to profess any creed are the professors in the faculty of divinity, who must all be ordained ministers of the Church of Scotland by law established. We were supposed to attend the college chapel on Sundays, and this many did and many did not; those belonging to the Dissenting churches frequented their own Bethels, which included the Scottish Episcopal Church.

The first four years (1889–1893) were spent in attendance at the classes in the faculty of arts, and in October of the latter year I entered the divinity hall, armed with a cautious testimonial from my parish minister (who chanced to be my father) to the effect that, "so far as was known to him," there was nothing as to my character inconsistent with the profession to which I was being called.

At this point I had for companion in my lodgings a student of the same year, who was supposed, like myself, to have a "call" to the ministry, and it was in reality he (now himself a minister of the Kirk) that gave me a taste for anything non-Presbyterian and set me on the road which led me at last to my proper destination.

Although a Presbyterian and the son of a Presbyterian minister, he was a great lover of the Episcopal Church, having lived most of his life in England and being familiar with all the rites and ceremonies of the Anglican Church. He explained to me the mysteries of the Book of Common Prayer and the various divisions of the Christian year, of all which I was then as innocent as the babe unborn; I liked it very much.

He was a High Churchman, so far as such a being can have any real existence in the Scottish Kirk, and, anxious doubtless for the conversion of his fellow-lodger, he did his best to imbue my mind with the same sentiments. He was tolerably successful, for, being by temperament inclined that way, I took kindly to High Church ideas and soon showed my sympathy with them. In the theological college, I think we were the only two that had leanings in that direction, and in a debate in the theological society we, as mover and seconder, were able to carry by one vote the affirmative side in the question, "Is Union with Rome Desirable?" For arguments to back up our audacity we consulted the local priest, himself a distinguished convert from Anglicanism and now gone to his reward.

Our professors were a heterogeneous company, theologically speaking. Three were irreproachably orthodox and inexpressibly dull. A fourth was an iconoclastic radical who dished up the philosophy of ecclesiastical history made in Germany, while the professor of biblical criticism, personally devout and delightful, was so advanced as to be practically indistinguishable from a Unitarian.

This being the condition of matters in the professorial chairs, one may imagine without difficulty the effect upon those occupying the benches. We were rooted and grounded in no particular faith. There was no system in the teaching and no unity. The lectures and textbooks on the various subjects were either so vague and indefinite or so unsatisfactory and destructive that I really did not know where I stood or how I could give a coherent account of the creed we were supposed to uphold. We got scraps of different things, but no consistent or logical whole, such as is presented to the Catholic seminarist in his philosophical and theological training.

Here is the great contrast between the Catholic and Protestant preparation of young aspirants to the sacred ministry. Prescinding even from the intrinsic error or truth of either system, one thing at least is certain: The Catholic Levite has not the least doubt what doctrines he has to believe, what is meant by them, and how they can be proved; the system (granting the foundation) is absolutely flawless and impregnable; it is a beautiful and unimprovable unity. The Protestant, on the other hand, after all his training may, and often does, find himself in intellectual and spiritual confusion; all is so changeable, undefined, and contradictory. It could not be otherwise in a college where the color of the teaching depends upon the particular "school" of the professor.

The same is true of the Scottish universities—indeed, we may say, of all Protestant universities everywhere. Students are sent forth indoctrinated with the views of that professor who happens to teach with the most brilliancy and persuasiveness; in the present instance it was naturally the quasi-Unitarian professor who captivated the intellects of the majority of the budding divines. In general, of course, we were all Presbyterians and could swear, and were obliged to swear, to the "confession of faith" (with reservations); we confessed the great "fundamentals" of the Christian religion and were prepared at all costs to champion the Church of Scotland. But within these bounds there was a wide field for developing theological speculation, and even at this early stage there were among us adherents of the three distinct parties: High and Low and Broad.

Yet it never occurred to me at this period that there was anything seriously to object to in our "Auld Kirk." I attended its "diets of worship" always on the Sundays, partook of the Lord's Supper at intervals, and as often as possible "sat under" a literary and ritualistic minister, to whose sermons, full of wit, pathos, and instruction, it was a real delight to listen.

I took my share also in teaching a Sunday school during the session and addressing meetings in mission halls and occasionally gave pulpit supply at a weekend. After the service on one of these adventures, I was tackled by a layman regarding my sermon, which, he alleged, ignored or impugned the divinity of our Lord. From this I gather that I must at this time have been superficially affected by the rationalistic teaching in the college. I know that I read a good deal of Renan and was carried away by a kind of enthusiasm for the brilliant Frenchman, whose style is so insidious and whose theories are so dangerous, especially to the susceptible and ignorant.

It was customary, too, for divinity students to plead, in parish churches during the summer vacation, for funds for the missionary society of the universities. This task I undertook once, but only once, for, on reporting that my expenses amounted to twelve shillings and the collection to eight shillings six pence. I received no second invitation.

It was during my last year and a half as a student that I got my earliest acquaintance with, and liking for, things Catholic and Roman. I was very friendly with a fellow student, De M., who was not generally known to be a Catholic. Besides himself there was only one other Catholic student, and that was the son of a Church of Scotland clergyman, who had renounced his living and, along with wife and family, had embraced the faith.

De M. persuaded me to go with him to the local chapel for Benediction, and the impression of that Benediction service can never be effaced. I understood, of course, nothing of it, except the sermon and the English hymns. I thought, as many outsiders think, that the priest had a little bell concealed beneath the veil, which he rung as he swung round. But the whole sight was to me supremely touching and beautiful. Bejeweled ladies kneeling side by side with swarthy toilers (a thing I never saw in any Presbyterian kirk), the many lights, the little surpliced boys, the clouds of incense, the tinkling bell, the sweet hymns, the supernatural stillness—all went home. I revisited the church on various occasions, though never for Mass, and took others with me (so contagious is the "glamour of Rome") and always liked it.

The whole style of Rome, both in her discipline and her worship, began to appeal to me. I had a sneaking kind of reverence, moreover, for that strange, mysterious, impenetrable person, the priest, and was inclined to think that, as a spiritual functionary, he was certainly ahead of our ministers. As an instance of this, I felt instinctively that the proper man to bless the little bronze crosses which I had bought was Fr. A, though I could not have explained why, and the bare suggestion greatly annoyed one of my Presbyterian friends, who claimed that ministers could bless them every bit as well. The fact that Presbyterian ministers as a body reject such blessings as the rankest superstition and profess themselves incapable of doing such a thing of course made no difference to him.

These bronze crosses, I may here remark (one for each of us), I bought at a Catholic repository in Edinburgh when passing through that city, which I had to do on my way home for holidays. It was a High Church thing to wear a cross at your watch-chain, to have a silk hat with extra broad brim (you might be taken for a bishop or at least a dean), and to get your coat made with tails almost touching your ankles. After visiting this shop, I would pop into the cathedral just opposite—more for the purpose, I am afraid, of looking at all the popish objects and of buying some Catholic Truth Society pamphlets than of praying.

Of the Real Presence, of course, I then and for long afterward knew absolutely nothing, yet I always experienced in a Catholic church a strange feeling of awe and mystery which I never felt in any other. The pamphlets I devoured most eagerly, and they gave the first shock to my Presbyterian complacency. Year by year I bought more of them, till latterly I had quite a large collection. I am convinced there is no more effective method of undermining a respectable Protestant's prejudices, and dispelling his ignorance, than by getting him to take a regular course of these Catholic Truth Society pamphlets.

During the summer of 1902 I had charge of a little mission station near Edinburgh. One evening a "converted" Spaniard who called himself Rodriguez, along with his not-so-much converted wife, supplanted me as orators at the service by leave of the parish minister. They told of the "Lord's work" in Spain, where they were laboring for the conversion of the benighted inhabitants.

Rodriguez displayed a rosary and a large altar bread, which he said the Spaniards worshiped. Personally, I was disgusted (I hated ranting Evangelicalism of every kind) and so, I discovered, were others, especially with the bold female, for whom, says St. Paul, "it is a shame to speak in the church." What possessed me to ask the favor from the man I cannot tell, but I did ask for and obtained the altar bread, which was enclosed between two pieces of cardboard. For long I kept it, respectfully and carefully hidden away in a drawer. I was proud of my treasure and showed it to certain chosen friends; finally, I either consumed it or burned it. I am well pleased with what I did and thank God for the inspiration. So my Catholic sympathies grew and deepened, unaccountably I admit and to a large extent unconsciously, for I was still devoted to the Auld Kirk. But there was something always drawing me closer to the Roman Church. So far, I knew nothing of her except a little externally, but I was soon to be placed in circumstances which enabled me to get a better knowledge and to see a little into the interior.

Licentiate

My college studies (eight years) ended. I was licensed by the presbytery in March 1897 and became by courtesy "Reverend." Licensing (a kind of minor orders) entitles one to preach and visit the flock and bury people, but a licentiate may not administer the two Presbyterian sacraments, baptism and the Lord's Supper, or perform the marriage ceremony.

An appointment of this kind fell to me in the West of Scotland at Easter, under a dear old minister, who was, I think, on the whole, the most zealous and devout Christian outside the Catholic Church that I ever met. He labored, and had done so for about fifty years, night and day, with his whole soul and body, for God and his parishioners, according to his lights, and to the Catholic poor among them he was truly charitable. Had he been a priest, I am sure he would have emulated St. John Baptist de Rossi and the Blessed Curé d'Ars.

He was intensely Evangelical, and my popish leanings distressed him sorely. He believed and said that the Church of Rome was "sound on the Atonement"; her doctrine about the sacrifice of the cross pleased him; but for the rest, he held that she was Antichrist and the pope was the man of sin and that, broadly speaking, she fulfilled in her history the prophecies of St. Paul and St. John regarding the mystery of iniquity. He was probably the only minister in Scotland who honestly subscribed to every jot and tittle of the confession of faith in all its literalness. Obviously, my only hope of being in agreement with such a man was either to avoid religious subjects altogether (which was not very natural) or to denounce the Broad Churchmen (which was quite natural).

At this period I bought a good deal more Catholic literature, including books, Catholic Truth Society pamphlets, and the like, but my knowledge of things Catholic was widened principally by visiting the houses of the Catholics in the parish, who were colliers. I always delighted in entering their homes, speaking with them, and picking up what information I could about their faith and practice. With true Catholic civility, they were always respectful, though they were horny-handed sons of toil and I came to them as a wolf in sheep's clothing. I loved to see their holy pictures, crucifixes, rosaries, and other evidences of their faith.

The thing that struck me most of all was the distinctively religious atmosphere about their dwellings, even the poorest and most degraded. There might not be a stick of furniture in the house nor anything that you could truthfully call by the name of table or chair; the floor might be a mass of filth, the walls swarming with vermin, and the children all but naked; yet one thing you could never miss seeing—a picture of the Sacred Heart, or of our Blessed Lady, or of the pope, or some such emblem of religion.

There was in that house a belief in the supernatural, a devotion to a religious creed, a remembrance of the existence and the nearness of the next world, that you would look for in vain in Presbyterian houses. It was touching to see it, and it impressed me beyond measure.

"These people, at all events," I would say to myself, "do not forget eternity. Their religion perpetually reminds them of their relation to God; it lifts them above this sordid world and teaches them to remember the supernatural. It is not of the earth, earthy; it is not a religion for one day out of seven, like the Presbyterian; it is an everyday reality. It is not put on, but is a part of their very selves."

I could not, indeed, disguise from myself that many were living drunken lives, were continually appearing in the police courts for weekend offenses, and that the condition of their houses was an outrage on every principle of sanitation. I will confess that I was scandalized by much of what I saw, and I also had a fearful suspicion that all this was due to their religion. But, then, I found that many Protestants were every whit as bad and that it was precisely those Catholics who never went near the chapel either for Mass or confession that were the worst. I found, moreover, other Catholics practicing their religion who were models of virtue and piety.

I listened to their religious conversation and was edified. I learned of their love of God, of their reverence for all things sacred, their self-sacrifice, their unbounded devotion to the priest and their belief in his supernatural power, and their uncompromising refusal to associate with any other form of religion.

Somehow, all this seemed as if it had the true ring about it and looked like the genuine article. I was drawn to it in some ways and repelled in others. I could not understand it all. It appeared a strange mixture of good and evil. The most natural thing, in such a case, for a Scot and a Presbyterian and a limb of the Kirk, would have been to shrink back in loathing and hatred. But—thank God!—I was not deterred by any apparent evil from considering the matter thoroughly. I always tried to take the kindliest view of it.

As was to be expected, these Catholic sympathies often found expression in conversation with my aged superior, much to his alarm. At times I felt attracted toward the Anglican Church. I read the *Church Times* and bought some ritualistic publications and began to think (such was my confusion of mind) that perhaps in the Anglo-Catholic branch of the Church one might be able to have all Rome's beautiful things without her errors. I argued often on these lines, and many an argument we had on the subject. Plainly enough the old gentleman was saddened at my giving vent to High Church ideas, and wearing the bronze cross, and kneeling at prayer when conducting service. He said people were talking. I was not surprised, considering that I had a little oratory in my room, where a huge rosary was conspicuous, and that a large photo of Leo XIII in the act of blessing adorned my sitting-room. Our church service was of the baldest type, which harmonized well with the building itself. I felt a longing for something less tedious, but it was out of the question there, and any little ritualistic tricks on my own account were at once detected and denounced. Of course one might and did introduce, subtly, collects and prayers from the Book of Common Prayer and the Catholic Apostolic (Irvingite) Liturgy, and even from the Roman Missal (I had bought a copy of the *Missal for the Laity*). But all these were partly unintelligible and, where intelligible, were wholly unsuitable to a congregation at a Presbyterian service.

One night the old gentleman took me to task in his most severe manner, having heard I had "nearly gone over to Rome." This I had to deny, but added that it appeared to me that, so tremendous were her claims, Rome was either the true Church of Christ or else a huge imposture. He agreed and of course declared for the latter. Another night I remember saying, "I do not see how the Church of Christ could have gone wrong, as we are supposed to believe she did, for some centuries, considering the promises of our Lord that he would send the Holy Ghost to 'lead her into all truth' and that the gates of hell should never prevail against her." Clearly enough, I had been digesting some points of Catholic controversy.

I took the opportunity also, as often as possible, of visiting Catholic churches in Glasgow; one summer I spent some holidays in Ireland, where the sight of the faith and devotion of the people helped me on my Romeward way. I revisited the Isle of Saints once or twice afterward, while still a minister, and each time what I saw of the Catholic religion made me love it more and more.

It was on one of these trips that I bought a small two-penny picture of our Blessed Lady, at a mission at Caherdaniel, County Kerry. This little object of piety I thereafter always carried with me wherever I went, and I still preserve it, much damaged and blackened, as one of my greatest treasures. I have little doubt that the Mother of God rewarded this act of love toward her by obtaining for me the grace of conversion. Yet, after all this, I took fright and drew back for a season. Whether I was afraid of a public exposure of my popery or was terrified lest I should be doing wrong in letting myself go so far in the direction of Rome, I cannot now say for certain; but this much is certain: that on a sudden impulse one morning I made a bonfire of all my Catholic Truth Society pamphlets and other Catholic belongings, including, I am afraid, the picture of Leo XIII, half hoping that thus I might rid myself of the whole question.

But, as Cardinal Newman remarks, a man who has once seen a ghost can never be as though he had not seen one, and—thanks to Jesus and Mary!—the fire that burned the books could not burn the love and longing for Catholic doctrine and ritual out of my heart. I soon took courage again and in a short time gathered together as much as I had destroyed. At this point, too (1900), in the good providence of God, I obtained still better opportunities of inquiring into the Catholic system and familiarizing myself with Catholic belief and practice.

Inquiring

Having spent three years as assistant to the venerable clergyman aforesaid, I left at Easter 1900 to occupy a similar post in a fashionable parish in Glasgow. Here we had a fine church and a more "ornamental" service, with a choir costing £300 a year, which the congregation paid for and criticized. In such a city I was able, without let or hindrance, to satisfy my Catholic cravings by reading Catholic books and papers, speaking with Catholics, and visiting chapels. One little chapel in particular, belonging to the Jesuit Fathers, I used to frequent on Monday evenings at the Benediction hour.

The following summer, accompanied by a sister, I visited that truly Catholic land Belgium and saw all that was to be seen of Catholicism there. I was delighted beyond measure with the grand cathedrals and monasteries, the pictures and shrines, and all other external evidences of faith and devotion. Never shall I forget the impression made on me at seeing for the first time (what I had often read about) the poor being fed by the monks as in the ages of faith. As we approached the gate of the Cistercian monastery at Westmalle we beheld a crowd of beggars being supplied by a lay-brother with abundant rations. This, I knew, was what one would have seen in Scotland, too, in Catholic days, when the poor were honored and cared for by the religious orders, when the land was covered with houses of charity and mercy and beneficence, and every form of human want, misery, and sickness was relieved by the devoted men and women serving their Lord in the vows of religion.

Today, I thought, these unfortunate hungry souls would be hustled into a poorhouse, to eat the bread of charity extorted by taxation. On this occasion I gained the friendship of Fr. Hermann Joseph, then guest master, who assisted me by his prayers and letters during the next few critical years. The life of those Trappist monks, a continual oblation of themselves to Almighty God in silence and seclusion, far from the madding crowd and cut off from all that the world counts dear, struck me as supremely beautiful and holy. I wondered where, within the bounds of Protestantism, one could find such an example of love of God.

Looking back on those days, I seem to have been drawn toward the Church more on sentimental and aesthetic than on doctrinal grounds. I had, indeed, studied many Catholic books and controversial writings, such as those of Newman, Faber, McLaughlin, and Di Bruno, and had read piles of pamphlets. Much of my ignorance had been enlightened and many illusions dispelled.

In particular I was now convinced that many, if not most, of the stock accusations against the Church of Rome on the historical side were wholly false. Charge after charge about popes and monasteries, persecution and immorality, I had satisfied myself, was nothing but the merest calumny. I had never before heard any but the Protestant side of these questions; now, after due investigation, I began to see that the Catholic answer was complete and crushing. As the hoary fables against Rome handed down in pious Scottish families turned out, one by one, to be nothing but the baseless fabric of the Protestant imagination and to melt away into nothingness like snow before the sun, I began to wonder if the Protestant indictment contained any scrap of truth at all.

Still, I could not say that thus far I was conversant, except superficially, with Catholic theology. Assuredly, I could not have passed an examination in the *Catechism of Christian Doctrine*, nor had the question, "Is Rome right, after all, and am I bound to submit to her?" forced itself seriously upon my conscience.

Fortunately, however, in my new sphere I was to meet with two other clergymen of the Church of Scotland who had for long—indeed for much longer than I—been observing and studying the Catholic religion and whom I found to be deeper in love with it, and more dissatisfied with Presbyterianism, than I was myself. Likeminded as we were, and pursuing the same inquiry, we naturally met together often; from the discussions I learned much that was

new about Catholic history and doctrine—especially from one of
the two, who had for years been making a profound and extensive
study of the whole subject and had traveled in Catholic lands in the
course of his researches.

Now, as he, the chief of the *dramatis personae*, who was already
"ordained" (the other, like myself, was only "licensed"), became a
Catholic about two years before I did, and later a priest, and published in two successive volumes (*What Happened at St. Michael's*
and *Why I Left the Church of Scotland*) the whole story of those
precious days and an account of the reasons of his own submission,
I need not lengthen my narrative by covering the same ground
again. Briefly, however, I may sum up the results of the reunions
among us. For some time after our association together, we—the
highest of High Churchmen, of course—tried to persuade ourselves
that the ministers of the Established Church were really successors
of the apostles and of the pre-Reformation clergy and that there
had been no break in the continuity of the Church in Scotland. This
quaint notion on my part arose from mere ignorance.

Whatever the others may have thought, I certainly never imag-
ined that ministers either claimed or possessed the power to say
Mass or forgive sins. This single point of difference between the
old and the new Church in Scotland would have been enough in
itself to shatter all ideas of continuity in the mind of anyone that
had properly studied the question. But, as I said, I was ignorant and
confused. Notwithstanding the hopeless inconsistencies and absurdities of the whole position, I still tried to think that we were
really a branch of the Church Catholic and argued and even
preached in that strain.

After some time our meetings and researches and pilgrimages
began to produce the inevitable effect, and we found ourselves has-
tening on to an acceptance of almost all Roman doctrine. I say "pilgrimages" because we were used to pay pious visits to an old Celtic
chapel, now in ruins, not far from where the third of our party held
his assistantship. We rowed over to it in a boat and prayed there on
our knees within the desolated shrine and invoked the saints to help
us to know the truth and to get the strength and courage to embrace

it. Many a visit also we exchanged at one another's dwellings, and we felt, all of us, that the case was becoming desperate and demanded a settlement one way or another.

At this stage, I need hardly say, things had advanced so far that the English Church was put out of court altogether: It was a question either of the Scottish Kirk or Rome. No compromises, no half-measures, were thought of. The Anglican Church might boast of having bishops and altars, fasts and festivals, grand cathedrals and a solemn liturgy, but all these did not make her more Catholic than ourselves. They were merely externals.

If the Scotch Kirk was wrong, the English Church was just as wrong. We were both separated from Rome and both condemned by her. The English Church and its companion, the Scottish Episcopal Church, might arrogate and assume superiority over the Presbyterian body, and unchurch it, and claim to be the only Church of Christ in Scotland possessing valid orders, but the upsetting answer to that, of course, was Rome's judgment upon the Episcopalians. The fact of a jackdaw dressing itself out in peacock's feathers does not make it a peacock. If Rome was right, the English Church was a schismatical and a heretical body no less than the Scotch, though the latter showed less anxiety about the matter, and we should not better ourselves ecclesiastically by jumping from the frying pan into the fire. Hence the issue was, in one sense, simple and clear.

We were not misled—God be thanked!—by any Anglo-Catholic illusions or diverted out of our straight course by any specious arguments about national Catholicism. We saw quite clearly that, for a logical Scotch mind, the English Church was not, and could not be, a resting place, but only (if anything at all) a stepping stone across the stream, and it was better and wiser and safer, if any step was to be taken, that we should take the big jump right across, once for all. The great question was, "Is it necessary to take that jump?" So far as our "ordained" companion was concerned, he settled that question for himself in the affirmative in the autumn of 1901.

At Michaelmas we met, the three of us, by appointment, at the little ruined sanctuary of St. Michael, and there and then he made known to us his resolution to quit the Presbyterian Kirk forever and knock at the doors of the Church of Rome. We were not surprised at this decision, as it had for some time been evident that it was the only possible conclusion to which his studies and convictions could lead him.

For ourselves, neither of us was prepared to take so momentous a step, because we were not yet in conscience convinced that the change was necessary. I will not deny that I was on the point of following my friend to Rome and actually took some steps toward making my submission and led others to understand that I was going, but a great fear seized hold on me, lest perhaps I should not have given the matter enough consideration and study, lest I might be making a mistake, acting too impulsively, following a friend headlong, and taking a false step which might wreck my life. In a matter involving nothing less that one's eternal salvation, would delay not be wiser? Would it not be better to wait and see whether further prayer and study would not lead to a different conclusion?

Whether I acted rightly or wrongly at that crisis, God alone knows, but this I know: I acted according to my conscience, formed amid the most conflicting emotions and opposing influences. I was as yet, so I reasoned, only an unordained assistant; I had not come to the full bloom of my vocation, so to speak, supposing God had intended me to be a minister of the Kirk. Perhaps I had not given myself a full chance of working out my salvation in the state wherein I was born. Perhaps it had been intended by Providence that I should be ordained in the Presbyterian Kirk and have a parish of my own, where I should be in supreme command, and administer the sacraments, and have the full responsibility of souls, and be kept busy, and interest myself in all the work of the parish. Perhaps then I might see matters in a different light theologically and feel quite happy. To leave the Church of Scotland at present might really be to condemn it without knowing it in its perfection. In any case, to postpone decision till I arrived at greater certainty surely could not be wrong. Then at least I could have no regrets, and it would serve only to make the final judgment more solid and lasting.

Influenced by these considerations, I remained where I was, as did my companion in distress. We promised, however, both to him who had taken the heroic step and to each other that we should keep the question open, that we should study and pray and be faithful to God's light and grace and not allow any worldly motives to influence our judgment for an instant.

To this determination I think I may safely say we were faithful, shutting out of view every consideration except that of our eternal salvation. Thus we parted from our friend who had resolved to leave all and follow Christ. I saw him not again until the happy day when he welcomed me on the platform of the station at Rome as an aspirant to the priesthood, toward which he himself had already taken the first steps.

Objections

That I still continued to turn my affections toward Rome and gradually to lose confidence in my own position may be gathered from the remark I made about this time to a professor of church history, who was generally supposed to be training his students to be Catholics of the Scotch Presbyterian type. This ritualistic gentleman, anxious to prevent a "perversion" to Rome, was arguing that, although the Kirk had many blots and defects and had lost much through the extreme violence of the Reformation, yet she would remedy that some day soon and would recover her bishops and sacraments and liturgy and prayers for the dead and things of that nature and that meantime the loss of all these did not destroy her identity with the pre-Reformation and the apostolic Church.

"Suppose," he added, doubtless thinking this an incontrovertible analogy, "suppose, for example, Mr. D., you lost an arm or a leg. Well, it would be a great pity, but you know you would still be the same Mr. D. for all that." "Yes," said D., "but suppose you lost your head? What then?" He was silent, and little wonder, for that was precisely what the Church in Scotland had done in the sixteenth century: It had lost its head.

Another argument our High Church brethren employed to try to persuade us to stay and be faithful to the Church of Scotland was that it was cowardly to leave it simply because we thought it defective in some points; it was mean to abandon it when so much was to be done in the way of repairing the breaches and restoring old Catholic doctrines and practices. Far better surely, more noble and dutiful, to remain and take one's share in rebuilding the shattered walls of the national Jerusalem and making her Catholic again.

Meantime what of one's own soul? If we believed that we could not be saved in the Kirk, how on earth could we stop in it? Nothing was left but to go out and get into the right train. Were we to lose our souls by stopping in a false church on the plea of trying to restore Catholicity within it, which really meant foisting popery on unwilling and bewildered Presbyterian congregations and causing no end of friction among the poor, stupefied old Protestants of Scotland? The truth is that such a proposal was based entirely on the notion that all these Catholic things, while very nice and desirable and devotional, were not at all necessary for salvation.

The suggestion could have come only from ritualists—from men who loved ceremonial and ritual display and would have it introduced wherever the people liked it or, worse still, whether people liked it or not—but who failed to go down to the root of the matter and to see the necessity of belonging to the one true Church, of believing each and all of its doctrines, and of submitting to its discipline and government. On us, therefore, these appeals to sentiment and loyalty made no impression whatsoever. We did not believe that one could be saved equally well in any Church and that the only difference was a matter of "millinery and incense." We could not conscientiously jeopardize our salvation on the score of Catholicizing a Presbyterian Kirk. Each one of us had an individual soul to save and to save in the way in which Almighty God willed it to be saved.

Hence the question narrowed itself down to this: Where is the true Church which Jesus Christ founded? Wherever it is, we must belong to it. If we find the Kirk is wrong, we must leave it, no matter how much we love it or with how many and deep ties we are bound to it. Our Lord's words cannot be trifled with: "If any man come to me and hate not his father and mother and wife and children and brethren and sisters, yea, and his own life also, he cannot be my disciple" (Luke 14:26).

One difficulty that might suggest itself to the mind of the reader is worth noticing. How, he may ask, could you reconcile your position with loyalty to the Church of Scotland or even with common honesty? If you were disgusted with it and had ceased to believe in some at least of its principles, how could you remain one of its ministers? I answer: Because I was a Protestant and was entitled to use my private judgment respecting Christian doctrine and principles, because I was not positively certain that the Kirk was absolutely wrong, and therefore I was not obliged to leave it, and lastly because I was only acting as did many others who rejected large portions of the creed of the Kirk and yet continued to minister in its pulpits with perfect equanimity.

For the most part, I confined myself to preaching those dogmas which were accepted by most "orthodox" Christians. Nobody pretended to believe every part of the "confession of faith," which was and is the doctrinal standard of the Presbyterian churches. Indeed, I had heard distinguished members of the General Assembly (the supreme legislative court of the Church) impugning some of the chief Calvinistic doctrines set forth in the "confession," such as those dealing with the fatherhood of God, election, and the like.

There was all manner of different "schools" within the ample fold of the Establishment, beginning from the lowest Evangelical who was almost a Salvationist, continuing with the skeptical Broad Churchman, who might believe anything or nothing, and ending with the papistical High Churchman, who hated the name Protestant and went as far as he dared in the direction of Rome or at least of Canterbury. Everybody—at all events, every minister—knew this was the state of matters. There could, therefore, be no dishonesty or hypocrisy in a searcher after truth like myself (who might be classified in the third category) hanging on to the Kirk as long as he could.

Assuredly, such confusion, chaos, and contradiction in matters of religious belief must, to every Catholic, appear a perfect travesty of the Christianity founded by our divine Lord. He thinks of the tens of thousands of priests and the hundreds of millions of lay folks in the bosom of the Catholic Church absolutely united in their religious tenets and submitting as one man to her authority in questions of faith and morals. He knows that any one of these, whether priest or layman, who should dare to disbelieve or doubt or deny a single article of defined doctrine would straightway be guilty of a grave sin against God and would be cut off as a dead branch and would be good for nothing but to be cast out and trodden under the feet of men and cast into the fire.

Such a thing as a priest presuming to pick and choose among the Church's doctrines and yet being suffered to act and speak as a priest is a thing simply unthinkable. The reason, of course, is plain enough. It is because in the Catholic Church we have infallible authority on the one hand and supernatural faith on the other. She is the teacher sent from God, and her children, knowing her to be such, believe her teaching with divine faith. In the Protestant bodies it is far otherwise. Their ministers and members do not believe their church is a teacher sent from God, and they acknowledge no infallible authority except the Bible, interpreted by each one's individual judgment. Practically speaking, therefore, among them there is no such sin as a sin against faith interiorly, just as there is no such sin as a sin against authority exteriorly. There is no fixed, definite, circumscribed, cut-and-dried body of religious truths which must be believed under pain of sin. Truth is progressive and changes and advances with the march of ages.

If you object, "But you must believe in the 'confession of faith' to which you signed your name," you receive for answer: "That is a secondary standard of belief; it is subordinate to the Bible; it is infallible only so far as it agrees with the Bible—and of that I am the judge and no one else. I am not to be tied down hand and foot to a document which represents the opinions of one man in the sixteenth century. Much has happened to modify Christian belief since then, and it would be bondage and servitude of the worst type to bind my intellect to accept a creed which sets forth the passing notions of Calvinism in a time of religious confusion and revolution. I adhere to the Presbyterian system and accept in general the 'fundamental truths' common to all Evangelical Christians, but beyond that there is an ample field for liberty of thought, and this liberty, as I allow it to others, I claim for myself."

Within a church with such elastic sides, anyone can see that there might be found the most divergent views and that no one could cast a stone at his neighbor and call him heretic. There could hardly be such a charge as that of dishonesty brought against any minister, be he High or Low or Broad. Everybody, strictly speaking, was dishonest, so far as the "confession" was concerned, and hence it might be said that, in that case, nobody was dishonest. There was a general agreement that the document was antiquated and unbearable as a final statement of Christian doctrine, and the Kirk, as a matter of fact, has often discussed the question of how best to relieve the minds of ministers from its incubus.

All that was left to a man, then, in such a state of doubt and flux was to hold on by the Bible in default of any more satisfactory authority. As I flattered myself that I really believed in the Bible and all its parts more literally and simply and genuinely than many of my clerical brethren, I failed to see why I had not as much right as they to hang on to the Church of Scotland till better days should dawn and the clouds should be rolled away.

Parish Minister

Following close upon my resolution to delay proceedings for a time and take to prayer and study came an appointment as parish minister. Scotch folks elect their pastor by popular vote. It may seem funny to a Catholic that the sheep should choose the shepherd. But, then, a minister is not really a shepherd in the sense in which we Catholics understand it; he is rather the president or chairman of a religious society whose members are more or less united in the same views and aims and agree to make him their head. In this sense the popular election of a minister is not so incongruous as it would appear at first sight and is certainly much more reasonable than the old system of lay patronage which was abolished in 1874.

I had then to stand this popular election test. Five or six candidates preached and prayed on successive Sundays before the congregation at E.; and, on a vote being taken, it was found that I had more votes than the others put together; hence I was elected. This shows how ridiculous is the method of taking a man's popular preaching as a test of his fitness for the ministry of a parish. Most Presbyterian clergymen read their sermons off like an essay. Now, the Scotch infinitely prefer a sermon delivered without manuscript, just as they prefer—in fact, will hardly tolerate anything else than—prayers delivered without book or manuscript.

So it happens that the candidate who has either the "gift of the gab" (to use a slightly vulgar expression) or the gift of a good memory and can declaim his sermon in an apparently extempore manner will be almost certain to carry the day. Once in, he cannot be put out, except for heresy or immorality. Heresy is a thing of the past. Immorality is not, but the expenses of a libel action are so great that Scotch folks are unwilling to undertake it.

It would be a waste of time to detail all the steps that followed the election and culminated in my installation in the parish—the "taking on trial" by the presbytery, the ordination, the "laying on of hands," the luncheon, and the presentation in the evening. I was supremely thankful when the ceremonies were ended.

There was everything in my new sphere to make me happy and contented in the Church of Scotland, if happiness was to be found in it at all. A simple and hospitable people to minister to; a beautiful district; a fine house, with plenty of glebeland round it, a huge garden, and ample salary, all more suited for a man with a wife and six children than for a miserable bachelor—these are a few of the things that might have made anyone happy who wished to be. After all, these were merely external comforts and could not reach a man's soul, if he cared about his soul, and if a man's soul is not at peace with God, no amount of exterior comfort or wealth or luxury can possibly make him happy. On the other hand, a man might be in direst poverty, yet, if he were interiorly tranquil, he need not envy the happiness of an angel. Such was the conclusion that forced itself upon me after I had spent some time in my new surroundings.

I was still unhappy. Ordination, the full charge of a parish, and the care of the souls I found were no remedies for my troubles.

At first, and indeed for a considerable period (although I was parish minister for only about twenty months in all), hard work kept me from worrying much. But the haunting dread that I was in the wrong ship never left me and at length began again to reassert itself with its old strength. I prayed night and day for God's help to see the truth and faithfully to follow it whenever found. Latterly I invoked (with fear and trembling lest I should be doing wrong) the Mother of God, whose picture I had exposed in various rooms. I read much Catholic literature, as before, and studied the controversy in all its details. I often had consultations and discussions with my friend B., whom I visited from time to time. He knew the controversy more thoroughly than I and could enlighten me on many points.

I spent holidays in that most Catholic land, Ireland. I took every opportunity, both there and in Scotland, of visiting Catholic churches and studying the working of the system on the minds of its people. In my visitations I entered the Catholic houses and was well received, and I exhorted them to go to Mass and be staunch to their faith. The priest afterwards said I had acted as a curate to him! So much attracted was I by the Catholic services and doctrine that, even when I had preached in a Presbyterian church in the morning, I would, if I could, go in the evening and assist at Benediction and hear a Catholic sermon.

An interesting experience in this way befell me in Edinburgh. I had preached in an Established church on the Blessed Trinity. In the evening I attended St. Mary's Catholic Cathedral, where I heard Canon Donlevy (whom God rest!) preach about the first Council of Jerusalem and its decrees, and, as it was the week of the sittings of the General Assembly of the Presbyterian churches, he was able to draw an amusing and highly striking contrast between the binding force of the decrees of Catholic councils and the utter uselessness and invalidity of the decisions of the General Assembly, which bind no one, whether minister or "elder," any further than he wants to be bound. This was precisely the position of the church in which

I was unfortunately situated: There was no authority, and consequently there was naught but confusion, disunity, and chaos.

After many months of anxious and prayerful study, of investigation of the question on every conceivable side—without consulting any Catholic priest, impelled only by a desire and determination to arrive at some definite conclusion, absolutely uninfluenced by any human or earthly consideration—I came to the conviction that I was wrong. The church I was in was wrong; she was not the true Church, the historical Church of Christianity; she was a modern invention, and her creed and her worship, the work of John Calvin and John Knox, were things the like of which, I was convinced, had never, till the sixteenth century, been seen either in heaven above or on the earth beneath or in the waters underneath the earth. What were the arguments and considerations that led me thus painfully to this conclusion? To begin with, the first and most damning fact that impressed itself upon me was the utter disunity among Protestants, the multiplicity of sects and divisions, the chaotic condition of Christianity outside of Rome. I was quite sure, from what I read in the Bible and from the whole conception of the Christian revelation as delivered by Jesus Christ, that his true Church must be one, that there could not be two true churches teaching contradictory doctrines, and, whatever modern indifferentists might find it convenient to say in their excuse, still it could not be really true that one religion was as good as another, and Almighty God never meant it so.

Not only did I see various churches and sects warring against each other and holding contradictory opinions, but I found each church at war with itself. I knew, for example, beyond doubt that even in my own church there were three distinct schools of theology and that I actually had relatives, and near relatives too (clergymen), who believed and taught differently from what I believed and taught. Yet we belonged to the same church and were supposed to have sworn that we believed the same "confession."

This was a spectacle and a state of things which I felt, and knew from my study, had no parallel or sanction in the days of the apostles, or in the days of the early Church, or indeed in any succeeding century till the sixteenth. It was the creation of the Reformation and was a thwarting and opposing of the will of Christ. The church, then, by whatsoever name it might be known, exhibiting this blot and defect, could lay no claim to be part of that body of Christians for whom Jesus Christ prayed "that they all may be one," concerning whom he declared there must be "one faith, one baptism," and to whom Paul wrote that "if even an angel from heaven preached any other gospel than that which had been preached to them, let him be accursed." I turned to the "sister Church of England" and saw the same desolating spectacle; indeed, I saw a worse spectacle in some respects. Bad as the Church of Scotland was, she had a final authority within herself. In the matter of deciding questions of dogma or ritual, the General Assembly was the supreme tribunal, and from this there was no appeal to any higher court.

Much as the English Church boasted of her apostolical succession and her "incomparable liturgy," the supreme deciding arbiter of her doctrinal and ritual disputes was the Privy Council, and the Privy Council was a body composed of men who might be Christians, Jews, infidels, heretics, or atheists. That a committee of such persons, of any belief or of no belief, should have the power, and should use it, of pronouncing infallibly upon matters of Christian dogma and worship was the climax of absurdity. Yet the English wished it so. The king was their head in all things, spiritual as well as temporal.

But a step further led me to see the cause of all this chaos and division: It was the setting up of the Bible as the ultimate authority in religion. This I came gradually to see was no ultimate authority at all. The Bible was never meant to be the sole and self-sufficient guide to men in learning the revelation of Almighty God. It could not possibly have been the authority at a time when it did not exist as a Bible; it was not fitted to be an authority for all, for it was a difficult book to understand, and, as a matter of fact, it led to the most divergent and incompatible conclusions. Each sect staked its opinion upon the Bible, yet each was different from the other.

The Protestant attitude to this book was, therefore, a wrong attitude. The Reformers gave it a false place in God's economy of dealing with men: Having abolished an infallible Church, they set up an infallible Bible. But, unfortunately, the Bible is only an infallible guide if you can tell infallibly what it means, and this is what you cannot do, as Almighty God has not gifted private individuals with the attribute of infallibility.

Daily I saw the deplorable evils into which an unlicensed and irresponsible interpretation of the Holy Scriptures had led the people in Scotland and became sick to death of the arrogance, confidence, and self-righteousness with which each little "sectling" would demonstrate from "the Book" that it and it only was right. Division and subdivision into all manner of sects and meeting-houses had followed the principle of "the Bible and the Bible only."

In two out of the three parishes in which I had labored I had known of houses divided against themselves—the father going to one meeting and the mother to another—and of the congregation of "the Lord's people" consisting of one family only. Doubtless they considered that, because the Lord had spoken of the "little flock," therefore they were likely to correspond to it. The Bible, then, I discovered to be a thoroughly unsatisfactory and impossible rule of faith, yet to the Protestant churches it was the be-all and the end-all of their existence.

In the Wrong

Again, on the historical side, the Presbyterian Church hopelessly broke down. It was quite clear to me, from the evidence of Scripture itself, as well as the whole nature of God's revelation in his Son, that he had founded a Church to which he had committed his truth to be preserved and perpetuated till the end of time, that this truth was a definite, recognizable body of doctrines, and that his Church must have been endowed with the power of guarding and teaching and handing down this truth. Wherever this Church was to be found, it assuredly could not be the Church of Scotland, which came into existence only in 1560, which contained relatively a mere handful of members, and which taught conflicting and fluctuating opinions instead of "the faith once delivered to the saints." I could not persuade myself that the Kirk was the Church founded by our divine Lord on the day of Pentecost, and, if it was not that, it was nothing. It was a small sectarian institution adopted by one nation in an out-of-the-way corner of the earth, but it was condemned alike by the Greeks and Anglican schismatics and by Rome. Its psalm-singing and Kirk session and Lord's Supper and barren worship and hideous churches, and its whole system of doctrine and ceremonies, were, as I said before, a new thing upon the earth: an invention of certain men to propagate newly-discovered opinions in the sixteenth century—opinions which are now being discarded and growing old-fashioned.

It could by no possibility be identified with the Church of the apostles, the Church of the Fathers, the Church of the early and later Middle Ages, or the Church existing in Scotland and Europe before the Reformation. Its theologians and textbooks claimed for it that it was thoroughly scriptural, that it was based upon and could be supported by the Gospels, Acts, and the epistles of Paul. This I could not admit; but, even supposing so much were granted, it would not be enough. A church to be the true Church of Christ must continue and persevere and preserve its identity, must develop and subsist all through the centuries. The Church was intended to be perpetuated from age to age, living and growing and extending, yet ever the same, teaching the same truths, keeping up an unbroken continuity and succession, according to the promise of its Founder that the gates of hell should not prevail against it and that he should be with it always.

This continuous succession and history of preservation, of course, the Presbyterian Church could not show and made no attempt to show. Indeed, the great boast was that the Church had become incurably corrupt, both in doctrine and morals, for many centuries and that, through the labors and genius of heaven-inspired prophets such as Calvin and Knox, the true gospel had been discovered again and the true Church of God set up in Scotland. Such a claim as this, to my thinking, condemned Presbyterianism out and out. A church which was compelled to skip over many centuries and jump back, over the heads of saints and Doctors and Fathers, right into the Acts of the Apostles to find its origin, repudiating and rejecting all that intervened, could not conceivably be the institution that our Lord meant to continue throughout all ages and to stand out as a witness in every century for his revealed doctrine.

"Take care, young man!" said an aged doctor of divinity to me, when discussing this point. "Once you get into the Fathers, like Newman you are on an inclined plane that leads right into Rome." It is perfectly true, but it cannot be helped. The Fathers must be reckoned with, for they represent the development of the Christian Church and present to us Christian doctrine as it came down from the apostles. If a church in the nineteenth or twentieth century could not square its doctrines with those of the Fathers, then it should at once give up its claim to be apostolic.

The Presbyterian Church, needless to say, threw the Fathers overboard, because it was sadly conscious that their doctrines and hers were irreconcilably at variance. Historically, she was a thing of yesterday. All our forefathers before the Reformation in Scotland were Catholics. If I had been living then, I should have been a Catholic too. The saints that looked out at me from the pictures, whether in my own house or in Catholic churches, were all Catholics and would not recognize me as a member of the same body as themselves. I should be reckoned an alien, an outcast, and a heretic. I could claim no spiritual kinship with them, no communion with them, no share in their prayers and labors and sanctity. What a horrible thing, to be cut off from all lot and part in the sanctity of all the ages!

The glorious cathedrals and monasteries and abbeys and churches, whose ruins abounded in every part of this unfortunate land, were all witnesses to a different faith from mine. They were built by the pious labor of priest, monk, and layman, who believed in abbeys and monasteries and in the conventual and monastic system—who were in short Catholics. What they believed in then all the Christian world believed in also. Scotland was not Protestant at that period: She was Catholic and had never been aught but Catholic. Her ecclesiastical pedigree ran back right to the time of

Ninian and Columba and Mungo, who had preached a faith that was Roman and Catholic, for at that age there was no other. In the sixteenth century, therefore, there had been a religious somersault; the only thing to be done was to take a somersault back again.

But I am going a little too fast. It was one thing to be convinced your own church was wrong; it was another thing to be sure which one was right. That it was necessary to belong to the true Church to save one's soul, I was perfectly certain; that I could not save my soul in the Presbyterian Church I was equally certain. Thousands of others, because they were not disturbed in their conscience, and saw no reason to change their belief, might be in good faith. But I was not in that position. I had entered upon an inquiry and was bound before God to pursue it to the uttermost, come what might.

In the meantime I should simply stay where I was, holding what truth there was in the Church of Scotland and officiating for the people until I was convinced that it was sinful and dangerous to remain longer. So long as I had not made up my mind that some other particular church was the true Church of Christ, I considered I was doing the only wise thing in stopping where I was.

I know that I offended some by preaching un-Presbyterian sermons and uttering Catholic sentiments which were abhorrent to them, for some expressed resentment at it, and probably many more felt resentment who gave no expression to it. I found that simple Scotch folks such as I had to deal with would bear with much before voicing their objection. Doubtless, too, many persons were offended when I indulged in certain ritualistic practices connected with the administration of the sacraments, the celebration of marriage, and the furnishing of the church. I have since learned that immediately after my departure they removed some objectionable objects, such as a popish-looking communion table, a missal stand, and other "relics of superstition."

One can perfectly understand their objecting to me or any minister trying to foist upon a simple Presbyterian flock ritual and doctrines against which it was the very object of their existence to protest and to get rid of which was the chief purpose of their revolt from Rome. We were not paid for doing that. Much blood had been spilled, and many fierce battles had been fought, and "covenants" entered into to banish such things from the land. Little wonder, then, that people should object to the introduction again of the thin end of the wedge of this hateful thing and ask themselves if their minister was attempting to undo, in as subtle a way as possible, the glorious work of reformation and of cleansing, to effect which their fathers had bled and died. (I repeat, they were entitled so to complain. They had every right to be protected from one who should aim at forcing upon them rites and ceremonies and beliefs which they detested and which did nothing but cause distraction, disharmony, and disedification. To this extent they had reason to complain of me.) Yet they complained as little as possible and were friendly to the very last. I quite believe they "thought furiously," but, excepting one or two, they said nothing.

By the grace of God and the intercession of his Blessed Mother, I was enabled to free the people from the incubus of a Romanizing incumbent—or "encumbrance," as *Punch* makes a country bumpkin call his vicar—and to find that peace and satisfaction for which my soul was longing. Day by day I felt myself further and further alienated from the Presbyterian, and indeed from the entire Protestant, ideal and system. It came at last to be a settled conviction that the whole conception of Christianity in the Protestant sense was utterly vitiated and wrong, and I was like a fish out of water in the midst of it. There was no rest for my soul day or night, and the solution of this most painful dilemma and perplexity was the subject that absorbed all my thoughts from the moment I rose in the morning till the hour that I retired. Some definite conclusion, and that a speedy one, was absolutely necessary to put me out of pain. Every argument and consideration that I could think of pointed to one Church, and to no other, as the ultimate authority that could solve all my difficulties, and that was the Catholic and Roman Church.

I have used the word "authority." I have felt the need of this. Everyone feels the need of authority, though, unhappily, not all look to the same authority or to the right one. Some, like Rationalists, take reason for their sole authority for everything; others, like the Evangelicals, take the Bible; but an authority of some kind everyone must have. I was clearly convinced that the authority for me was one that could teach me with infallible certainty and leave me in no doubt whatsoever as to the great truths about salvation. I wanted to have certainty, and I believed that Almighty God meant mankind to have it. Some good friends, in arguing on the point, would fain have persuaded me that this was an erroneous and unhealthy craving on my part, that God never meant we should have this kind of absolute certainty, and that Rome's claim to put us in possession of all necessary truth, without possibility of error, was false and delusive and pernicious, leading simple souls astray with its glamour and plausibility.

I could never agree with persons who took up that position. To me it seemed that the Incarnation of the Son of God, and his sojourn among men, and his teaching his apostles and declaring God's truth to them, and his founding a Church would have been superfluous and absurd and useless if he had not intended that men should be taught with unerring certainty what to believe. The very object and purpose of his coming down from heaven was to give men certainty about God and their relation to him, both in the present and for the future. To leave them, then, still in doubt and uncertainty, pursuing after the truth, struggling to find it out, confessing that they really could not take it upon themselves to say with absolute confidence whether or not this or that doctrine was true—all this struck me as making void the work and word of Jesus Christ, as stultifying and nullifying the teaching authority of our divine Master. If this were the true view of Christianity, then it appeared to me that men were in little better case now than they were before Christ came at all.

An authority, therefore, teaching with divinely-protected inerrancy, which could assure me that this was false and that was true, with the same certainty as our Lord assured his companions—for I felt that we had as much right to certainty in matters of religion as the first disciples—this was what I wanted. Precisely this was what no Protestant authority gave me, what, in fact, they expressly declared they could not give. This seemed to them almost anticipating the last day when the Messiah would "come and tell us all things." There was much, they said, in regard to which we must be content to remain in the dark, much that was obscure and uncertain and would be cleared up only in heaven. I did not want to be in the dark about anything when I thought I could be in possession of the light. I had been in the dark long enough—about thirty years, to be precise. I knew that the true Light had come into the world, enlightening all who wished to be enlightened. I felt certain that that Light, so far from shining with dazzling brilliancy for thirty-three years and then being extinguished, was shining still as brilliantly, to illuminate my darkness, if only I could come to it. As it was not shining in the Protestant church, the probability was that it was to be found in the Catholic Church. At all events the Catholic Church was the only Christian body on earth that claimed to have the light and the truth and to give it with infallible certainty. That was so much in her favor, to begin with, so much to attract the inquiring and dissatisfied soul, for a sick man turns away from a physician who proclaims his incapacity to cure him and appeals to the doctor who claims that he has a remedy that will prove effectual.

Examining, then, the "claims of Rome," I saw, from my reading of history, that she was the only Church that could reasonably and plausibly pretend to speak with authority, because she was the only one that could trace her ascent back to the apostles. She was emphatically apostolic. You could tell the day and the place and the circumstances of the rise of every other church in history and could name the very men who took the foremost part in founding it. But you could not point to any date or place when the Catholic Church took its origin except that occasion when our Lord said to Peter: "Thou art Peter, and on this rock I will build my Church." Here was a Church which came to me with a genealogy that could not be questioned, which could trace her family history back to Jesus Christ himself, which could justly boast of an unbroken, continuous growth from the seed to the great tree and from childhood to manhood. There was solid, matter-of-fact proof on hand of her genuineness and antiquity.

The illustration that Mr. W. H. Mallock used to support her claims in his book *Doctrine and Doctrinal Disruption* seemed to me singularly bright and conclusive. In that remarkable volume, in which, with ruthless logic, he makes mincemeat of the Anglican claim to speak in the name of doctrinal Christianity, he pictures the Church of Rome as "not a mere aggregate of undifferentiated units, but a living organism with a single enduring personality"—an organism like that of a human being, growing from childhood to boyhood, from boyhood to manhood, still preserving the same individuality through all development and growth and possessing a memory that never fails.

"Being endowed," he says, "with a single brain, the Church is endowed also with a continuous historic memory, is constantly able to explain and restate doctrine and to attest, as though from personal experience, the facts of its earliest history. Is doubt thrown on the Resurrection and Ascension of Christ? The Church of Rome replies: 'I was at the door of the sepulchre myself. My eyes saw the Lord come forth. My eyes saw the cloud receive him.' Is doubt thrown on Christ's miraculous birth? The Church of Rome replies: 'I can attest the fact, even if no other witness can, for the angel said: "Hail!" in my ear as well as Mary's.' " Such appeared to me the precise position of the Catholic Church in the world today, and no other church known to me could advance any title in the faintest degree resembling it. What confirmed me in this view of Rome's claim was the clear and unmistakable fact of her supremacy over the whole Christian Church from the earliest times. I took a long time to see this, but at length I could resist the evidence no longer. Anglican controversialists such as Puller (in his *Primitive Saints and the See of Rome*) try hard to disprove the universal headship of the Roman Church in the early centuries, but the arguments and evidence in support of it, brought together in such books as the reply of Fr. Luke Rivington and the work of Allies, seemed to me overwhelming.

Over every part of the Church Catholic, both East and West, Rome stood forth as not only claiming but as exercising jurisdiction, and her jurisdiction was obeyed. She would not have been obeyed had she not the right and title of apostolic authority to be obeyed. It was a right and a power and a privilege inherent in the See of

Rome, the See of Blessed Peter, to rule and govern the universal flock of Christ. Every bishop of the Catholic Church was, indeed, a true successor of the apostles and had a flock committed to his jurisdiction, for the ruling and feeding of which he was responsible. But his jurisdiction he derived from, and held in submission to, the bishop of Rome, the prince of the apostles. To be in communion with him was the test of orthodoxy; to "speak with the successor of the Fisherman" was to be in the true Church. What had been then continued to be now.

Our Lord's provision for the government of his Church and the preservation of the faith had undergone no change. It was as necessary today as in primitive times to be united with those whom our Lord had set in authority. Now, it could only have been by the will of God, effected by the Holy Ghost who came at Pentecost, that Rome should have acquired the supremacy over the whole Church, that the external government of the body of Christ should have assumed this particular form and organization, and that the preservation of the gospel in its entirety and purity should have been indissolubly bound up with the bishop of Rome. The Church, considering the promises, explicit and unconditional, of our divine Redeemer, could not have gone so far wrong as to lapse into this mistake. He had pledged his word that he would be with her always and that the Holy Spirit would lead her into all the truth.

The supremacy of Rome, then, was a matter of divine ordering and had been believed to be such from apostolic and sub-apostolic days. The fact that some had revolted and cut themselves off from her authority in no way invalidated her prerogative. Nothing was left, therefore, for me but to get myself in line with the rest of Christendom and get into the Bark of Peter, which, like that of Noah, was launched to save them that would be saved. Where Peter was, there was Christ, for it was from Peter's boat that Christ taught.

Besides, I saw plainly that unity, which was to be a mark of the true Church and which our Lord had absolutely willed and required among his disciples, never had been and never could be secured in any other way than by the supreme authority of the Roman Pontiff. Some of my friends—indeed most of those with whom I argued the point—scoffed at the necessity of unity, in Rome's sense, declared our Savior never intended such unity of dogma and of worship, and asserted that such a uniformity and unanimity meant degradation, stagnation in the intellect, and paralysis in the soul. It was, they said, the peace and unity such as one sees in a cemetery.

Presuming that unity was demanded by Jesus Christ, as I believed it was, I saw that, as a matter of historical fact, it never existed out of the Roman communion. No other plan or means of attaining to it had ever succeeded, and experience told me that what had been the fate of other methods in the past would similarly overtake those devised by men in time to come: Nothing but the supreme, independent, irreformable judgment of one man, and that the bishop of Rome in his office as Vicar of Christ and the successor of Peter, could preserve the union of the faithful which the Founder of Christianity willed his religion to possess.

It was, of course, a stupendous power and authority to attribute to one man alone—the power of declaring and defining what was the revealed truth of Almighty God and of binding the consciences of all men under pain of mortal sin to believe and accept his decision—a decision not reversible by the judgment of any other court, not to be submitted to any other tribunal for correction or approval, but a final, authoritative, independent, infallible decision, against which no man dare appeal. So great, indeed, was this power that it would have been utterly blasphemous and a glaring usurpation of the divine attribute to invest with it any man on earth who had not been unmistakably singled out by God to receive it.

This was what I believed about the pope: that he was truly the successor of Peter, whom our Lord had appointed head of the Church, to rule and teach and guide it and that, to do so effectually and perfectly, this gift of infallible authority was absolutely necessary.

Without this, his authority would have been in reality no authority at all; there would have been no unity. Who believes the archbishop of Canterbury to be infallible? Who believes the whole united Episcopal Bench in England (if you can imagine the Bench united) to be infallible? Who believes the General Assembly of the

Presbyterian Church, or the Union of the Baptist Church, to be infallible? The very question is ludicrous. What is the consequence? No authority that is worth the name.

What follows this? Chaos, confusion, division, disunity on the most vital and fundamental matters, each man is a law to himself and does that which seems right in his own eyes. If there is agreement among them, it is accidental, and it happens, not because any authority has spoken on the subject, but because the same ideas chance to commend themselves to different people. As I said before, this is a state of things which pleases millions; this is Protestantism—freedom from all authority except your own, intellectual liberty or license to think out doctrines for yourself. This, they say, is far nobler and higher than a compulsory unity. It is certainly a pleasant creed to profess and a popular creed, one that flatters human nature and human pride, panders to self-conceit, and frees a man from all subjection to external authority. On these terms, a man may believe anything or nothing, may stroll through life, so to speak, a religious libertine.

In my eyes the fatal drawback about this so plausible position was that it was utterly opposed to the will of Christ, to his intention, to his teaching. I could not believe that he meant Protestantism to be the ideal of his religion. I did believe that he intended every Christian to hold precisely the same truths, the same set of doctrines, and that these must always be the same, must be unchangeable, and all for the simple reason that he himself had descended from heaven to teach a certain set of truths, that these truths were, of course, divine and could never be altered, and that anything and everything different from these truths must be false.

The truths of Christianity, I held, could no more change than the truths of arithmetic; if they were true yesterday, they must be true today and tomorrow and forever. To change them meant that they must be susceptible of change and of improvement, and, if that were so, they might never have been true at all. Once grasp the fact that Jesus Christ was a divine teacher, was God in the flesh, and then his every word was divine, and divinely true, and true for all eternity. Hence it followed that his teaching must be a unity, that no part of it could be in contradiction to any other part, for truth is one—error only is manifold.

This was the Catholic conception of Christ's mission as a teacher, and it appealed to me as the true and noble conception. The Protestant conception was false and dishonoring.

On examining the claim of the Catholic Church to unity, I saw it could stand the most searching investigation. No doctrine of hers in one century ever came into conflict with her doctrine in any other century. No pope had ever contradicted another pope on matters of faith and morals. You could not discover such a case.

True, some plausible instances to the contrary were trumped up by Rome's opponents, but, on careful and conscientious examination, I found that they broke down, were capable of a perfectly reasonable explanation, and did not at all affect the claim of the Catholic Church to have set forth unity of doctrine before the world from the day of Pentecost to the latest pronouncement of pope or council.

Now, this was obviously quite supernatural; no human institution could stand such a test, could have produced such a record. That the Church of Rome all through these centuries, with such vicissitudes and trials, both without and within, dealing with such profound subjects as matters of eternal truth, should never have stumbled into the least error or self-contradiction was to me an indisputable proof that she had been divinely guarded and preserved. Only the finger of the right hand of the Most High could have brought her through unscathed.

On the other hand, I looked at Protestantism. Her career even for three centuries had been a record of variations, denials, changes, contradictions; she was split into a thousand fragments and was splitting into more. Herein was her condemnation. It was a necessity of her very being. It was just as necessary a consequence of her principles that she should be disunited as it was a consequence of Rome's principles that she could not be disunited. Unity was to me a beautiful, a heavenly thing; our Lord demanded it, and only in Catholicism could it be realized, only through the unerring voice of Rome's head, the Vicar of Christ.

Nearing the Goal

Over and above the conclusive proofs of Rome's God-given supremacy and authority, I examined and saw for myself that all her doctrines were beautiful and reasonable and attractive. Theoretically, of course, the proper thing to be done by an inquirer after the true Church is first of all to find out where the true Church is by the evidences of credibility, as they are called, to search and discover, by historical proofs, by Christ's promises, by the four marks and other lines of investigation, where lies that Church which the Son of God set up upon this earth, and, having found it, submit to it and believe all that it teaches, convinced that, being infallible, it cannot teach aught except what Christ taught. As a matter of fact, however, I suspect that the majority of inquirers do not pursue this method, logical and consistent though it be; there are too many difficulties and stumbling blocks to be got rid of first. There is a whole lifetime of ignorance and suspicion and delusion and bigotry to be undone. The trees must first be cut down and the ground cleared before one can set about building the edifice of Catholic truth. Hence for the most part I think that converts who wish to be intellectually convinced and are really in earnest about the matter examine each of Rome's doctrines one by one, and sift them, and try them by Scripture, and see whether they are reasonable or not. They also find it necessary to investigate the truth or falsehood of the most common charges and accusations against Rome's historical record, such as those of persecution, immorality, dishonesty, and the like.

I admit that, in a certain sense, this method is putting the cart before the horse, because many doctrines and practices which might appear strange and repellent to one still trusting only to his reason would assume quite a different aspect and seem altogether reasonable and holy after the inquirer had received the gift of divine and Catholic faith. An outsider, to put the matter plainly, is really no judge of the Catholic interior. Nevertheless, this method (of examining each doctrine singly) has decided advantages, and this I felt, and feel now, very much to my consolation.

The common Protestant idea about the affair is that a man becomes a Catholic, somehow or other, hypnotized and deluded by Rome's "glamour." Then he is obliged to assent to all the most ridiculous and unreasonable doctrines; he has simply to open his mouth, shut his eyes, and swallow everything wholesale: He becomes, in fact, a driveling nonentity, in a state of mental stupefaction and paralysis, compelled against his will to express his formal belief in things which are too silly and childish for any man of average intellect.

Brought up in heresy and trained by the tradition of generations to look on the Catholic teaching as both irrational and unscriptural, I discovered from personally investigating every item of it that, so far from being of this nature each was, when properly understood, lovely and reasonable and satisfying. I could even see the necessity of much of it, if the Christian faith was to be consistent. Though the Catholic Church declared that all her doctrines were matters of revelation, still, none of them, so far as I could see, was contrary to reason, but rather every one of them had a solid foundation in reason, and none of them was opposed to any part of the teaching of Holy Scripture.

On the contrary, many passages of Scripture which, taken by themselves, were meaningless or at least unintelligible became clothed with significance and consistency when understood in the light of the Catholic faith and interpretation. Even those doctrines of the Roman Church most ridiculed and attacked by Protestants—such as those dealing with the religious life, the priesthood, the pope, purgatory, confession, the Bible, and the Mass—assumed a beauty hitherto undreamed of, and the fact that her doctrines were all beautiful and holy and elevating to the soul was a proof that she must be the true Church.

It required a long time, I confess, and much discussion and thrashing out of the pros and cons of the case before I could see through indulgences and intercession of the saints and before I convinced myself that the undeniable prosperity, in temporal things, of Protestant countries, and their seeming superiority in that respect to Catholic nations, was really no argument against the divinity of the Catholic Church. Each convert seems to have his own particular stumbling-blocks according to his bent of mind or his upbringing or his previous study, and what troubles one doubting soul may never cause the least difficulty to another. I see now perfectly well that I was judging of this temporal prosperity question and many other questions from a thoroughly wrong standpoint and that if I had considered the matter purely from the point of view of a Christian instead of a Scotsman, I should have reached the correct solution sooner.

Furthermore, as I think I hinted before, I found that the gravest charges against Rome, whether in regard to her popes, her clergy, her religious, or her influence on people's lives, were, for the most part, wholly false, always misleading, and very often deliberate inventions of notorious enemies.

In the publications of the Catholic Truth Society and other controversial literature the scandals and falsehoods and calumnies were exposed in fine style and in a manner that satisfied me that the Catholic Church was the only Christian body now existing which fulfilled our divine Lord's prophecy about the persecution and slander that would overtake his true disciples. She and she alone was everywhere spoken against, like the company of Christians after Pentecost and during the earliest centuries. This appeared a mark of her divine origin. What was true in the charges made against her was nothing else than what one might expect in any institution that had a human side and was composed of frail men and women, while, on the other hand, the fact that she had survived and prospered and progressed in spite of the weaknesses and wickedness of her members and officials proved that she had a divine side, as no other body had.

I will not deny that I saw and heard things that scandalized me in the Catholic Church and in the lives of Catholics. Some of them, I now admit, were not a just cause of scandal, while others were. I knew nothing, at that time, of "pharisaical scandal" and the "scandal of the weak" and other distinctions drawn in moral theology. I should have suffered much less anxiety and doubt had I been acquainted with them. When all was said and done, I perceived that if there were any corruption or disedification, it was accidental and incidental and was in no way owing to the teaching of the Church, but in spite of it, and that the most attractive and edifying and devout characters were always those who were staunch papists and were faithfully practicing their religion and observing its every precept. When Catholics were good people, it was because they were good Catholics—their religion made them good. On the other hand, if a Protestant was a good man, it was not because he was a good Protestant first: His religion had nothing to do with it; he was better, indeed, than his creed, which a Catholic could never be. Herein was a proof of the sublime influence of Catholicism.

Last of all—for I am not writing a treatise on the proofs for the divinity of the Catholic Church, but merely recalling as best I can the main points that appealed to me in her favor—I will confess that the worship of the Roman Church drew me as much as her doctrine. I did not at that time understand the meaning of it all or perceive the significance of the various details of the ritual, yet I loved it and was impressed by it; there was about it a sanctifying, soothing, elevating influence that was to be experienced nowhere else.

I would pay visits secretly to Catholic chapels and remain for long, attracted by some mysterious power, subdued by the air of reverence and awe that always seemed to pervade the building, watching the lamp flickering in the sanctuary and the faithful stealing out and in with silent adoration. How I envied their faith! How I marveled at their devotion and reverence and profound seriousness! Religion appeared to be a real living thing to them; to most Protestants, on the contrary, their religion was a thing put on and off like their Sunday clothes. It was not a habitual, integral part of their daily life, as was the Catholic's.

Then, how grand and inspiring was the ceremonial of Mass and Benediction! I assisted at both the one and the other in various places, and, I repeat, I could not have explained what they were, but I felt there was a grandeur and solemnity about them, a hallowing and uplifting influence, that was utterly lacking in the dreary meetings of Presbyterians. The very buildings themselves were holy and edifying and true "houses of prayer," and, where the Catholics could afford it, they were obviously meant to be as worthy of the majesty of God as poor mortals could make them. The kirks of the Scotch people were little better than four walls and a roof and seemed designed on the principle that, however grand might be the houses of the rich, anything that would accommodate a congregation in comfort was good enough to be a temple of the Most High. In this certainly they were consistent enough, as they did not, and do not, believe that God "dwelleth in temples made with hands"; they hold that no one place is more sacred than another, seeing that God is everywhere, and consider that the main functions to be performed in a church is the preaching of sermons. On these grounds, naturally enough, it comes about that the chief thing considered in the kirks is not the glory of God, but the convenience of the minister and the people. This was abhorrent to my ideas of Christian worship, but it was Protestant.

I am persuaded now that what drew me into these sweet chapels, and moved my heart and captivated my love, and made me feel so happy, yet so mystified and awestruck, as I sat or knelt and stared at the tabernacle or the stations or the images and wondered and meditated, was nothing less than the Real Presence of our Blessed Lord, who was there watching me and drawing me to him.

What has happened to me in this particular has happened to many another. "There hath stood One in the midst of you whom you know not" is as literally true of non-Catholics visiting a Catholic church as it was true of the Jews in the time of our Lord. Only when they have received the gift of faith do they realize what was that silent, strong, irresistible Power that drew them to the altar as the magnet draws the steel and constrained them to abide there till the Incarnate God himself had wounded their hearts with the darts of his love. But was it right to love such worship? Was it not too sensuous? Was this not the "fatal glamour" of Rome which we were so often warned against? Did it not appeal too much to the emotions and the sentiments? Was it not too splendid and gorgeous? Was it not mere outward show? Was it lawful to allow one's aesthetic and musical taste to be ravished and carried away by such fascinating and overpowering ceremonial? Should we not, according to our Lord himself, "worship God in spirit and in truth"?

I have purposely crammed into these queries all the common stock-in-trade of Protestant objections to Catholic worship—objections sometimes felt, too, by timorous and scrupulous inquirers— not in order that I may refute them one by one, but that I may put on record the fact that they troubled me for a time, that I came to see through the fallacies with which they bristled on every side, and that I may dispose of them in a summary manner, in the hope that perchance some doubting soul may be encouraged also to look them boldly in the face and pierce through their hollowness.

The "glamour of Rome"! Of course there is a glamour. How could it be otherwise? Is it wrong that there should be a glamour about anything? Take a great orator or a great preacher who captivates and, as it were, electrifies his hearers, who seems to emit a kind of magnetism that draws and fascinates the audience that hangs upon his lips. Is that wrong? No: It is a gift from God. Why, then, should you object to the glamour and attractiveness about the worship of the Roman Church—I mean merely on natural grounds? Must it be wrong because it is beautiful? Are not beauty and loveliness and harmony creations of Almighty God? Must the worship of the true Church be hideous and repellent and bare and dreary?

Doubtless, in the eyes of those who have reduced the practice of ugliness in church building and church worship to a perfect science, it will seem most heinous to worship the Lord in the holiness of beauty, as in the "beauty of holiness." But sensible people unwarped by prejudice will confess that God is pleased with beautiful things and that the worship of the Most High is not any the more likely to be acceptable to him because it is ugly and monotonous and mean. The worship of the Church of Rome must be beautiful and fascinating, because it is the true worship; all the works of God are perfect. Heretical worship is hideous, because it is false. Truth is lovely, but error is ugly. The ritual of the Mass could not possibly be aught but sublime and beautiful because it has been fashioned by the Holy Ghost to be the one true worship in God's one true Church. The same may be said of all the authorized ceremonial of the Catholic Church for all her liturgical services: It enshrines and adorns the inward offering of the faithful; it is the setting, the framework, so to call it, encircling some doctrinal truth, some revealed truth of God; it is the divinely appointed ceremony and form of giving back to God that which he himself first taught us. It is the belief of Catholics (as it is a fact) that Almighty God has shown us not only the right faith, but also the right form of worship. He has prescribed a method of offering him public adoration. He has not left us to haphazard or chance. Mass, then, is the liturgy that Almighty God has willed as the chief act of Christian worship, and we have no right to attempt any other. Must it not, therefore, be lovely and attractive? Surely! There is a glamour about it! If there were not, it would indeed be surprising.

The One Fold

Should we allow ourselves to be affected by what appeals so much to the senses? Strange though it must appear to those who have been born in the Catholic Church, I have heard this question asked with much anxiety by intelligent and well-disposed Protestants. You might imagine, from the query, that we were pure spirits and not in possession of a body at all, without ears and eyes and other senses and faculties by which we appreciate material things. Is music wrong? Is painting wrong? In themselves, certainly not. Well, then, are they wrong when employed in the worship of our Creator? Again, no. Why should they be? Has God given us an artistic and aesthetic sense, a faculty of enjoying and being moved by sensible objects, and yet declared it wrong to satisfy these senses and operate with these faculties?

Primarily, of course, all the grandeur and beauty about Catholic worship is designed to give glory to God and magnify his praise. We consider it but fitting that all the treasures of art and music and ceremonial should be impressed into the service of our Maker. But if, incidentally and as it were by way of secondary consequence, the worshipers themselves are moved and fascinated and pleased by the worship, is that wrong? Are we to be doomed forever to a form of service that lacerates our feelings, violates our aesthetic and musical taste, and outrages every recognized principle of beauty and orderliness?

Thank God, many non-Catholics have been brought into the true fold through the sublime and heavenly ritual that Rome has composed century by century, under the guidance of the Holy Ghost! It was God's own way of bringing them in; then they came to see that the interior worship of God, the true doctrines, the life of sacrifice in the Church, were even more beautiful than the external ceremonial which had attracted them. They learned that only in Catholicity are fulfilled Christ's words that his followers would worship him "in spirit and in truth." There is no contradiction between outward splendor in ritual and the inward worship of the soul. If there were, how could thousands of persons of the greatest sanctity have loved it and been united to their Lord through it? Men could be sincere and earnest and devoted worshipers of Almighty God in "spirit and in truth," assisting at a pontifical High Mass, while, on the contrary, a man might be offending God, "drawing near with his lips while his heart was far away," when attending a Presbyterian meeting house.

I came to the conclusion, therefore, that the Protestant objections to the beautiful in Rome's worship sprang from false principles in regard to the nature of worship and the nature of man, from a prolonged bondage to the falsities of Calvinism, which had crushed out all love for the sweet and beautiful and attractive. Yet so firmly ingrained in my mind was the notion that, somehow, one could not be genuinely worshiping God with the heart in the midst of so much gorgeous ceremony, and that the Catholic was spending all his devotion on forms and ritual, that I required a long time to emancipate myself from such a delusion.

The truth I now know to be precisely the reverse—namely, that as a matter of fact, much of the Protestant service is nothing but a respectable lip service, a mere form to be gone through once a week for the sake of appearance, whereas the worship of the Catholic is the heart's adoration, presented to God in the most beautiful and perfect manner imaginable. His ritual is fixed; he need never bother his head about it; his whole attention is given, free and undivided, to the inward worship in spirit and in truth, whether he is priest or layman. Here is unity of worship, for it is the same divine Sacrifice and the same liturgy the world over. But yet there is a most wondrous diversity along with it, for every soul has its own particular needs and desires and aspirations and presents them before God with its own words, so that the humble beggar kneeling obscurely in a corner of the great cathedral, who unites with the nobleman and the grand lady—aye, and with the bishop and the pope himself, if he be offering the Holy Sacrifice—is as much a worshiper apart and separate, and dear to the heart and the eye of God, as though there were no other in the wide world.

O truly sublime and wonderful worship of the Roman Catholic Church! Beautiful outwardly, beautiful inwardly, made according to the pattern God himself has shown, no marvel is it that so many distracted and tempest-tossed souls have been riveted and fascinated and consoled by it. No wonder that it should have satisfied their heart and their intellect as well as their senses, for Jesus Christ, "the Lamb slain from the foundation of the world," is in it. He is its glory and its beauty, here as in heaven. He is the center of the worship of the Catholic Church, for he is the Sacrifice of the Church. So it comes that half an hour of the Roman Mass excels all the worship of all the heretics throughout the world.

Home at Last

But now it is time to tell of the final act by which I gave effect to those convictions which forced themselves upon me with an urgency that was irresistible. Many an hour and many a day of fear and trembling and terror, lest I should be taking a wrong step, did I spend. What if, after all, the whole thing was a huge delusion? What if I took the "plunge" that was really irrevocable and found myself duped and befooled and miserable? What of my father, an aged minister broken in health through illness and in heart through bereavement? Years ago I had asked him: "Suppose I turned Roman Catholic?" "If you wish to break your father's heart, do so," was his answer.

What of beginning life over again, and giving up old friends, and tearing oneself up by the roots, and sitting down again at school and learning a new religion? What of all the publicity and fuss and distress and legal proceedings to be gone through in severing my connection with the Church of Scotland and cutting the ropes that bound me to my parish? These and a hundred other reflections that Satan inspired flooded my soul day by day. Could we—my friend B. and myself—not emigrate to some colony and there take the step which was so difficult to take at home?

No, that would be cowardly. I made bold to call upon the priest in the parish and ask him many questions, without, however, acquainting him with our exact position. He gave us all the answers we desired. His quiet, simple, lonely life in the little house beside the chapel seemed to me much more apostolic than that of the ministers with their wives and families. It was a life of poverty, of celibacy, of self-denial, of devotion—in short, a supernatural life—that found no parallel in the Protestant ministry. I always consoled myself with this thought. Catholicism looked so beautiful to one who understood it not, and saw it only from the outside; how much more beautiful would it be once we were inside and knew and understood it all!

My friend and I agreed that the hour had come for us both to act together—to pack up and go. We adopted the line of least resistance, which was that of taking the step first and then informing our relatives and the public afterward. By the experience of others we had come to know that this was the best way to avoid opposition, bitterness, and all attempts to persuade us to draw back. We straightway gave in our resignations. I got a special meeting of the presbytery called to deal with the matter. We visited a canon of the cathedral in Glasgow, who arranged for our reception at a Benedictine abbey. I found mountains of obstacles (as I supposed then) dissolving into molehills. God wondrously opens up the way straight in such cases.

I went to communicate the news to my aged father.

At first he was shocked and saddened. His hopes and intentions for my future were rudely shattered. He thought he would never see me again and that I would he bound to hold that he and all his were going straight to hell. But by next morning he regained his equanimity and (such is the philosophy of the Scotch) inquired whether I would be in need of funds to carry me on. He appreciated the argument I used wherewith to comfort him: that the step was going to make me happy and that he could not wish anything better for me than that I should be happy.

I was then suspended from my ministerial functions, awaiting the final decisions of the presbytery. Summoned before the reverend "fathers and brethren," I explained that I had made up my mind, and had "burned my boats," and that it was useless to argue—a thing which some of them showed a desire to do. They were sorry for me, and pitied me, and thought I was more or less demented, and said they would let me know what they were going to do with me. Meanwhile I arranged for my departure from the parish, preached farewell sermons (with difficulty), and said good-bye to some of my more intimate friends. They were all my friends still. Though regretting that my conscience had dictated such a step, they yet admitted that conscience must be supreme. Thus did all others whose acquaintanceship I valued. Some came to me and begged me to reconsider my decision and made all sorts of offers to induce me to remain, but, of course, in vain. I had steeled my heart against all such influences and determined that this time there should be no looking back. The moment had arrived to "leave my people and my father's house," and to love God and his Church above all things, and to take up the cross and follow Christ.

So soon as the newspapers inserted a notice of the impending "perversion," I was inundated with letters, books, pamphlets, entreaties, and all manner of terrifying literature, intended to stop me in my mad rush into the arms of Rome. Needless to say, most of it went into the wastepaper basket; to some of it I replied, in terms as firm and strong as were consistent with politeness; some of the book-stuffs I returned, uncut and unread.

Almighty God and his dear Mother helped me through the crisis and solved its difficulties in a way that now, looking back at it, seems quite miraculous. The good priest of the place, too—a German—assisted me with his counsel and his strong Catholic enthusiasm at a time when I was almost fainting and tempted sorely to turn back. He held me fast and kept me from falling. Never, so long as I live, shall I forget his share in helping to save my soul. This is a crisis of your life when you need a strong Catholic friend to be constantly beside you to keep the devil at bay, for never does the devil exert his infernal powers more subtly than at the hour when he sees a soul about to be rescued from heresy.

In due course I was solemnly "deposed from the holy ministry of the Church of Scotland," having my name called three times at the door of the presbytery with no response. I sold off, and, having for some weeks received hospitality and lodging from the canon aforementioned, was sent to Fort Augustus's Benedictine abbey for reception. Having satisfactorily passed an examination in the *Penny Catechism* and made other preparations, under the charge of Fr. Columba, himself a convert, I was received into the fold and made my First Communion on the feast of the Assumption.

Now my story (tedious, I am afraid, to many) is ended. I could fill many pages more with the record of these first glorious days as a Catholic. I could tell of the deep peace and comfort and satisfaction of those first confessions—the joy and consolation of my first Holy Communions, the ever-increasing delight and wonder at the new world of beauty and sanctity that gradually opened out before me, as I passed month after month of new feasts and fasts and observances and devotions. It was like being transported into a new and unexplored world. I felt as ignorant as a child of real Catholicity, and the experience of all the loveliness and sweetness and holiness of the Church surpassed my wildest imaginings.

But of this I have written elsewhere and shall not now repeat my impressions after I went to Rome to study for the priesthood. Enough if I have explained the steps and reasons that led me from Calvinism to Catholicity. From the moment of my conversion till now, not a single doubt have I entertained that the Catholic and

Roman Church and she alone is the true Church which our Lord set up on earth and that to be sure of salvation everyone must belong to her.

If all who have at any time harbored suspicions about their own religious beliefs would set to work and inquire and pursue their inquiry with a merciless determination to find at all costs the true faith! If they did so, Almighty God would give them light and grace to enable them to discover it and reward them with a peace that surpasseth all understanding. There are thousands of Protestants in Scotland who are naturally good, with the making of saints in their character, but who will never become saints because they have not the means of sanctity within their sect. They have not the machinery (so to put it) for turning out the article. A bird cannot fly without wings, nor can a Presbyterian ascend the ladder of perfection, supernaturally, without the sacraments of our Lord Jesus Christ.

Sad, indeed, it is that a nation so blessed and enriched by Providence in the natural order should yet remain in a lower level in the things of religion. But a better day is dawning. Scales are falling from the eyes of many, and not a few are returning to the fold from which their forefathers departed. God increase their number till, illumined with the light of the true faith, the whole of the people led astray by Calvin and Knox find their way back "from the Kirk to the Catholic Church"!

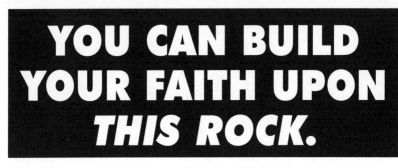

YOU CAN BUILD YOUR FAITH UPON *THIS ROCK.*

This Rock magazine brings you clear explanations of Catholic beliefs, field-tested tips on how to evangelize, answers to tough questions, and help in understanding Scripture. Articles are faithful to the entire body of Catholic teaching.

This Rock shows you how to prove Catholic beliefs using the Bible, early Christian writings, and logic, and it demonstrates why anti-Catholic charges are unscriptural—wonderful help for those with relatives or friends who have left the Church!

☑ Yes! Enter my one-year subscription (11 issues) to *This Rock*. I enclose $29.95 (US$44.95 to Can. and Mex., US$49.95 elsewhere).

Name _____

Address _____

City/State/Zip _____

Daytime telephone _____

❏ Check enclosed Charge my: ❏ MasterCard ❏ Visa ❏ Discover

Card # _____

Expiration date _____

Signature _____

TO ORDER CALL OUR TOLL-FREE ORDER LINE

1-888-291-8000 (credit card orders only)

OR MAIL THIS PAGE WITH YOUR PAYMENT TO:

**Catholic Answers
P.O. Box 17490
San Diego, CA 92177**

phone: 619-541-1131 fax: 619-541-1154 web: www.catholic.com

YOUR COPY
<u>FREE</u>

Pillar of Fire, Pillar of Truth **can turn lives around—whole parishes too!** It's the ideal introduction to the faith for Catholics and non-Catholics. Single copies are free to individuals who write to us directly. For multiple copies, see the chart below.

How to evangelize with *Pillar of Fire, Pillar of Truth*: Put copies in literature racks at church. Distribute them door-to-door in your neighborhood. Leave them at bus stops and other public places. Give copies to friends and relatives. Make a gift to your parish of a copy for each family.

QUANTITY	UNIT COST	TOTAL COST
1	FREE!	FREE!
2	$1.00	$2.00
100	$0.60	$60.00
200	$0.50	$100.00
500	$0.40	$200.00
1000	$0.30	$300.00

Prices include tax and shipping within the U.S.
For shipments to other countries, please contact us.

CALL OUR TOLL-FREE ORDER LINE
1-888-291-8000 (credit card orders only)

MAIL YOUR PAYMENT TO:
**Catholic Answers
P.O. Box 17490
San Diego, CA 92177**

phone: 619-541-1131 fax: 619-541-1154 web: www.catholic.com

HOW TO ORDER

Where We Got the Bible

If you enjoyed *Where We Got the Bible* (ISBN 1-888992-04-2), consider getting copies for friends. Each copy retails for $10.95. Shipping and handling are $4.95 for one copy, $5.95 for two copies, and $6.95 for three copies. (For shipping and handling on larger quantities or for foreign orders, please contact us.) California residents add 7.75% sales tax. Send your check or money order (U.S. funds only) to

Catholic Answers
P.O. Box 17490
San Diego, CA 92177

For credit card orders only, call toll free

1-888-291-8000

ATTENTION BOOKSTORES

Where We Got the Bible is available to bookstores at trade discount. Please telephone (619) 541-1131 or send fax inquiries to (619) 541-1154.

WHERE TO REACH CATHOLIC ANSWERS ON THE INTERNET

http://www.catholic.com